What leaders are s

Every leader is always looking f
make a greater difference in the (
him to serve. Piet Van Waarde has done all of us a tremendous favor in
sharing not only the opportunity to help our people to connect to God
but then that most important issue of discipleship of connecting with one
another. You will be blessed as you read this page turner, with someone
else in mind with whom this book needs to be recommended to. Read
and be blessed!

Johnny Hunt
President of the Southern Baptist Convention
Pastor, First Baptist Church of Woodstock

Piet Van Waarde captures the essence of the critical yearning that leads
people to put their trust in Jesus. It's authentic... real... and hopeful for
anyone willing to honestly look into the unsettled parts of their life. "
Jim Mellado
Executive Director
Willow Creek Association

No one chooses life's unsettling chapters. They appear unexpectedly. But
God is present in them. He can use them to break up a heart's hard soil
and to nurture fertile soil. Unsettled *begins with one person's journey.*
It traces the steps from a shocking awakening to trust and service. The
author's candid reflections on this journey will resonate with any who
would mine their own journeys for the godly wisdom that leads to witness
and worship.
David K. Clark, Ph.D.
Executive Vice President and Provost
Bethel University

If you're feeling unsettled spiritually or frustrated with yourself, then
read this book. In it, I believe you'll find a friend. Piet Van Waarde is a
gentle companion, someone you can be real with, who can help you get
meaningfully connected with God.
Sarah Sumner, Ph.D.
Dean of A.W. Tozer Theological Seminary

A winsome and very accessible guide for the journey of spiritual seeking...
Ruth Haley Barton
President, Transforming Center
Author of *Sacred Rhythms*

Piet Van Waarde's insightful book is a must-read for any seeker of truth, and provides a fresh look at today's concept of "faith." Anyone who has ever wondered if faith-finding/keeping is an outmoded or antiquated pastime will find fresh inspiration and compelling perspective in his honest, open discussion on the relevance of God in dealing with the complexities of our personal lives. Highly recommended!

Cindy Sheltmire
Missouri Film Commission

Piet Van Waarde is a friend of seekers. He has a sincere and passionate heart for those of us who wrestle with spiritual truth, and that heart is evident in every page of Unsettled. *With profound insight and tender compassion, he walks alongside those who are restless in the faith, and graciously provides both inspiration and practical help to equip us in taking the next tenuous step in our journey toward authentic relationship with a loving God.*

Elsa Colopy
Associate Editor *Focus on the Family Magazine*
Author of *A Woman Who Hurts,*
A God Who Heals

Unsettled *is a book that is both simple to read but profound in its message. From unbelief to understanding to living a life of faith, Piet has provided a road map for spiritual life. He has anticipated the questions that many will ask along this journey of faith and has given well thought through answers to the dilemmas we face. He avoids clichés responses to the difficulties of life and in contrast approaches problems with humility and authenticity. This book can be used as a powerful tool in the process of discipleship.*

Liz Swanson
Leadership Community Director-Recovery
Ministry Leadership Network

I believe that every really good book has two components. The first component is content relevant to life today. The second component is the courage of the author to be real; authentic. Piet not only shares very relevant content but he also is courageous enough to share his life's failures and findings. This book gives us all hope that, though we can't change the past, we don't have to be controlled by the past. Thanks Piet for inviting us into your life's journey. Everyone who embraces your content will connect with your courage and find the confidence to boldly move toward their future as you have done.

Mark Crow
Pastor, Victory Church.TV
Oklahoma City, OK

As a volunteer in the church and leader in the market place I find myself relating to people that are genuinely unsettled. I haven't felt confident about knowing how to respond—especially with those who are the most skeptical. As I read Unsettled, *I said out loud and often, "Yes! This is it. This is what I have been dealing with." Piet Van Waarde's book provides an authentic and realistic representation of our journey into a closer relationship with Christ; a journey filled with unexpected twists and turns. And yes, sometimes even with reluctance and regret. This book has given me vocabulary and perspective for continuing the soul conversation within myself and with others. I highly recommend this to anyone passionate about personal growth and ministry to people across the spiritual spectrum.*

Erica Pefferman
Vice President of Marketing, Zimmer Radio Group

Piet is one of the most gifted communicators I know. His words bring clarity and insight. His stories and life experiences are ones that we can all relate to. I thoroughly enjoyed Unsettled. *It is an inspiring and authentic reflection of the journey we all aspire to; from seeker to fully devoted follower. I felt both challenged and educated in the way God interacts with us and I'm sure it will have the same impact on you.*

Robert Koke
Senior Pastor Shoreline Church
President of ILM

Piet has communicated life-altering truth in a remarkably compelling manner. His spiritual wisdom and insights will bless new believers and long-time followers alike. As a person who has been on the journey for a while, I frequently found myself having "a-ha" moments. If your soul longs to evolve, don't miss this gem!

Craig J. Chval
The Chval Law Group, P.C.

This is a book that you will hand to friend or family member that is uncomfortable and doesn't know what to do about it. It's a captivating presentation of God's continual work in our lives, first to draw us to Him and then slowly heal and restore us to more accurately reflect the original image of His creation. It was a lovely reminder of the many times I have been unsettled in my life and God's faithfulness to use my uncomfortable, troubled feelings as a catalyst for showing me His love, faithfulness and intimate knowledge of my deepest needs.

Kay Yerkovich
Co-author of *How We Love*

As a Christian businessman I am always looking for a good book which explains the Christian faith in plain language. I love giving books to my colleagues and customers—and I heard this would be a great book for that—and it is! But, surprisingly enough it was a great book for me too. I think you will find that true for yourself as well. Read it! Love it! Pass it along!

Dan McNerney
CEO, Barnes Insurance Group

I have personally experienced the profound insight of Piet's teaching (as my pastor) for more than 5 years. As in everything he does, Piet gives Unsettled *his full heart, mind and soul in a spiritually sensitive and innovative way that truly addresses our deeper spiritual thoughts and questions. It is a timely fit for anyone wanting to look beyond the surface and explore the depths of who we are at our core. Regardless, if you are a student of Christianity or simply curious about spiritual matters, this book is a must read.*

David Perkin
Founder of the Perkin Foundation

If you are unwilling to settle for "good enough" in your spiritual formation process, then this book is for you! Piet has a rare knack for giving voice to what the Spirit is already whispering as true. Through story, metaphor, and concrete application Unsettled *will inspire you to take another step in your spiritual journey. Time and again you will find yourself saying: "I get it, I 'buy' it, and now I know how to apply it!"*

Dr. Rod Casey, DMin
Christian Formation Pastor
Woodcrest Chapel

UNSETTLED

life beyond the yellow ragged couch

BY PIET KOK VAN WAARDE

BRIDGE
LOGOS
FOUNDATION

Alachua, Florida 32615

Bridge-Logos
Alachua FL 32615 USA

Unsettled
By Piet Kok Van Waarde

For contact information, speaking schedule, and Piet's blog visit:
www.pietvanwaarde.com

Library of Congress Catalog Card Number: 2011934210
International Standard Book Number 978-1-61036-005-0

Printed in the United States of America.

~ DEDICATION~

To

my

oldest son,

whose journey created a measure of

unsettledness for some

but whose diligence

has become the reason

for hope

for many....

~ACKNOWLEDGEMENTS ~

No one can do anything truly significant by themselves.

Candidly, I feel somewhat disingenuous putting my name as the only name on the cover. Yes, I typed the words into the computer. The seminal ideas are my own. But this book simply would not be what it is without the contribution of many really incredible and selfless people. I'm not just being polite—that is the truth! I'd like to acknowledge at least a few of them here.

First, I want to thank Linda Fentress for planting this idea in my mind—or perhaps, better said, the Lord used Linda to confirm something that had already been stirring inside me. After a weekend service where I spoke on the topic of soul evolution, Linda unashamedly said, "Piet, this is an important topic. You need to write a book on this!" So the journey began. Isn't that how so many journeys begin? Someone says something that resonates with something already being considered, and the Spirit of God uses that comment to bring a dream to life.

Second, I want to thank the Pastoral Advisory team and the Board of Directors at Woodcrest Chapel in Columbia, Missouri. I am the lead pastor and primary teacher at this wonderful church. Writing this book took me out of the church and off the platform on multiple occasions over a four-year time span. They picked up the slack—joyfully so!

Third, I am grateful for Bridge-Logos and their team for taking a risk on me. I don't lead a nationally recognized church. I don't come from a large city. I haven't done a lot of outside speaking. But something about the subject and the way I wrote about it resonated with them and their team—and so they have taken the plunge with me. Specifically, I am grateful for the confidence and support of Lloyd and Peggy, Christy, my editor, and Susan with Word Productions LLC.

Finally, there are a number of individual contributions to the book that were absolutely strategic. My readers, Cindy Sheltmire, David VanDyke, Elsa Colopy, and Crystal Rodenbaugh—each one of them had timely and helpful commentary that contributed significantly to the work. Dr. Rod Casey, Craig Chval, and Dr. Sarah Sumner spent untold hours combing through the manuscript, unselfishly giving me the benefit of the brilliant minds. Teresa McBean wrote a Foreword that brought me to tears. Erica Pefferman was an enthusiastic cheerleader and consultant from the beginning. The McNerneys and the Perkins believed enough in the project to help bring necessary practical resources together. My wife Carol and children put up with many late nights with daddy/hubby behind the computer. Last, but certainly not least, there are those who graciously provided endorsements for the book—lending their name and credibility to an idea they thought might make a difference for good in the world. God's blessing on each of you!

Now, to Him who is able to do immeasurably more than anything we can ask or think, may He be pleased to use the words that follow to confirm His work in every unsettled soul that reads it!

~ FOREWORD ~

✦

When I was a younger believer, I longed for a book that would give me a roadmap for how to live a "good Christian life." I didn't find one. Eventually, I began to chafe under the message "*do this* and all will be well with your soul."

My life experiences were increasingly at odds with the testimonies I heard so often in church: "I was lost; then I was found. And now, *I'm fine*." I became frustrated at this poor substitute for the truth that I longed to hear. The reality is that my life was both Christian AND decidedly *not* fine. I had (and have) regrets. How could I reconcile these life experiences with the messages I heard? Where was the authenticity?

Therefore, I was delighted to discover this book. Within its pages are stories that resonated with my own spiritual pilgrimage: faith found in funny places alongside moments of simply wanting my own way no matter what. All of this coming together in a life marked by points of grace. I found within Piet's stories the promise of a meaningful and abundant life. I suspect that this book will encourage, inspire, and potentially reframe what it means to experience life transformation.

Whether the reader is seeking to get started on a spiritual path or is a longtime Christ-follower who wants to finish the walk authentically, this book is for everyone. It provides an honest roadmap, not ignoring or sidestepping the detours, hazards, and dead ends—nevertheless shining a bright light toward a path that leads unerringly toward authentic Christian-formation.

I love this book!

Teresa McBean, Executive Director
National Association for Christian Recovery
Coauthor of Bridges to Grace

~ CONTENTS ~

~ INTRODUCTION ~

The night is darkest just before the dawn. —Spanish Proverb

There are few things in life that are more troubling than the feeling of unsettledness. I think we have all felt it at some point. Probably more often than we care to admit. It is that feeling of being off balance, anxious, jumpy, and uneven. It isn't enough to take you out, but it is enough to keep you up. We know something is wrong, but we are not always sure what it is or what to do about it. It is . . . well . . . unsettling . . . .

Yesterday my son went back to rehab. Twenty-two hours ago he was checked into a twenty-one-day in-patient program for substance abuse. My wife and I don't know what to think. We feel very unsettled. But mostly we just feel numb.

It is his second time through. For the last two years, I thought he was doing better. He was in technical college. He loves computers. He has always been good at math. He called regularly. He came home for Christmas. He was working a part-time job and getting decent grades—or so we thought. The truth is, things were not as we thought.

I am the senior pastor of a larger congregation in our community. I love our church, but I love my family more. As a dad, I have been careful not to sacrifice my children on the altar of ministry. I worked hard at relational parenting. My wife was committed to full-time mothering. We were imperfect parents. But we believe we got the big things right. So how does one explain what is happening in the life of our oldest son?

I can't . . . at least not completely . . . .

For several years, I have felt words stirring inside me. They are words that I thought might be meant for a broader audience. I thought they might be my contribution to the larger work of God's

Kingdom. Perhaps they will be. But today I realize they are first and foremost for my son and people like him

My son went to a Christian school through grade four. At ten years old he made a personal commitment to Christ. He was baptized. He had some great youth leaders at church and spent summers at the best Christian camps in the country. Our son knows the Bible stories. He has heard the apologetic messages. He never resisted church. I think he actually liked it. As he entered high school, we completed a new state-of-the art youth space. Apparently, none of that was enough.

As God intended, we all have our own choices to make. We can't force people to "see the light." They have to want to see it. They have to see their own need for it. Something has to be stirring inside that says, "What I have been doing isn't enough! I need something more!"

We must become unsettled.

But do we know what to do with this feeling? Do we know what it means and what causes it? Do we only have to address it once and then we're good for the rest of our lives? What about those of us who have heard it all and have done some things well—and still struggle?

I think those of us whom God has called to pastor and teach must think of new ways to say things. Not to change the message, but to say it in a way that helps those who struggle, those who can't seem to shake the unsettledness. I think we also have to be more open about our own questions, doubts, and struggles.

The truth, of course, is that the message of Christ has always been a difficult message to live with. It has always been about laying down one's life. It has always been about doing the counterintuitive thing. Jesus challenged us all to pay attention to our souls, even when that was unpopular, inconvenient, and uncomfortable. So yes, it is hard for all of us. So in one sense we live in a perpetual state of unsettledness. The soul evolves reluctantly. Lord, help us!

The words in the chapters that follow were at one time simply an odd collection of personal musings, journal entries, and old sermon notes. I hope that they now come together to provide a perspective on the soul that gives you a reason for hope—a reason to do life differently. Perhaps God will graciously use these words to help you navigate whatever unsettledness you feel toward a more productive and useful end.

I pray this is so.

Piet Kok Van Waarde

MY STORY

TURNING

A person with divided loyalty is as unsettled as a wave of the sea that is blown and tossed by the wind. —James 1:6 NLT

My bus stop was only a block and a half away from my house. But on the third of September in 1968, it might as well have been a hundred miles.

I was sitting toward the front of the bus. The first seat, actually. A very uncool place to sit. But I knew what was coming, so I didn't care. Survival, at this point, was more important than coolness. The door to the bus opened much too slowly. Didn't the bus driver see the four guys in the back plotting my demise? I jumped off the bus and the four were on my heels. I lived on a dirt road, so while I was running they were trying to find rocks. I don't think I ever ran so fast. Apparently good rocks were hard to find. So by the time they found adequate ammunition, I was long gone. All they could do was make fun of my name. I had lived another day.

My given name was Pieter Kok. I was born in the Netherlands. My name is a common Dutch name. In the States—not so much. For most of my growing-up years, it was pronounced "Peter Cock." I dreaded the first day of school. The teacher would read through the list of names in the class, and I always knew when she had come to my name. There was a pause and then the hesitant pronunciation—then the giggles. I still wince when I think about it. Bus rides home weren't much fun, either. Kids with funny names apparently deserve to be chased home with rocks.

I changed my last name when I got married to a shortened form of my mother's maiden name. Consider it compassionate decision-making on behalf of my future kids.

Because I had a "different" last name growing up, I was often the brunt of crude jokes. I grew up with a battered soul. I tried desperately to be accepted, but never really fit in. Nothing seemed to work. I tried student government—but I was always soundly defeated. I tried baseball, but I was always one of those kids who was good enough to make the team, but not quite good enough to start. So eventually I just wanted to escape. Escaping worked for a while, but eventually that, too, left me unsettled and wanting more.

I still remember the night *that* came clear to me.

The stench of spilled bong juice filled the air. Half-empty beer cans were leaking around the trash can in the corner of my one bedroom apartment. It was 2:00 A.M. and I was sitting on a ragged yellow couch with my best friend, surveying the mess.

It was supposed to have been a small get-together, but word got out that there was a party at my place. Lots of people came—many I didn't know. Apparently people had fun; the trashed apartment was evidence of that. I don't remember much of the evening myself, because I had partaken in some strange mixture of microdot, hash, and beer—and my brain was very much in a fog. All I could think about was how long it would take to clean up the mess, and how much of the security deposit the repairs would confiscate.

It hurt to think.

In the midst of my stupor, Chuck (the only remaining partier) said, "Hey, Piet, we are always going to live like this!" He was excited about that prospect. For the first time in years, I was not. I don't know if it was the mess in the apartment, the frustration about cleaning up after a group of unwelcome freeloaders, or the aftereffects of too much partying and not enough sleep, but the fact was, I wanted out.

Chuck's words haunted me: "We're always going to live like *this*."

In the weeks leading up to the party, I had witnessed firsthand the real-life consequences of the so-called party life. Good friends were getting addicted to cocaine and stealing money to support their habit. Dealer friends were going to prison. I even found myself in a jail cell for an illegal joyride on a motorcycle without a license. This party life was no longer fun. I really didn't want to live like *this* anymore.

How do good people end up in places like this?

I was raised in a strong Christian home. We went to church regularly growing up. My parents required church attendance. I don't really remember hating it; I just didn't "get" it. It was part of the family routine; like good hygiene and going to school, we didn't argue about it, we just did it.

But in my later high school years, I could begin making my own choices, and I didn't see any reason to stay committed to a religious ideology that didn't allow kids to play baseball on Sunday. Why commit to a God who required that? I wanted to have fun. I wanted to be cool. That was what the party life promised. The warnings I received from parents and teachers about the dangers of drugs and drinking just seemed overdone. Many of my friends were using. We were just having a good time and It was a way for me to be part of the crowd.

Why not?

It took only four years of being in that scene to discover the emptiness and shallowness of it all. I didn't really want to live like *this* anymore. I became increasingly tired of the superficiality of it all. Richard Rohr put words to my thoughts: "We are circumference people with little access to the center. We live on the boundaries of our own lives—confusing edges with essence, too quickly claiming the superficial as substance."

The depth of my unsettledness put me in serious spiritual search mode. My brother, who was an active and enthusiastic Christ follower, perceived my curiosity and began sharing about the value and meaning of his faith walk. He eventually invited me to a Bible study, and I did the unthinkable—I accepted his invitation. Me! Cool Mister "Life of the Party Guy" attended a Bible study.

Surprisingly, this group of Christian young people showed me a side of Christianity that I found winsome and interesting. Faith, for them, wasn't about rules and rituals; rather it was alive and relevant in their everyday lives. The more I got to know them, the more intrigued I became about this Jesus who was so real to them. I prayed sincerely for the very first time in my adult life.

But even with the interesting conversations and compelling examples, I was still confused. I still wasn't sure. Could I walk away from the friends, the popularity, and the fun? I waffled back and forth for months.

Finally, on one particular Friday night, I found myself driving back to a familiar party scene, Seaside Park. My friends used to gather in the parking lot at the end of a long peninsula that jutted out into the Long Island Sound. That night I wasn't thinking as much about partying as I was thinking about God. I wanted to experience God, but I couldn't imagine myself breaking away from the life that seemed so normal for me—and everyone I knew. So, perhaps out of sheer habit alone, the car took me to this all-too-familiar party place.

While driving, I made an interesting observation. On one side of the car there was a beautiful sunset. I was taken by the colors, the clouds, and the seagulls. On the other side was the group I had been hanging with. Kids were on the hoods of their cars, smoking and drinking—the same spilled bong juice and beer cans scattered about. The scene that had so drawn me in a few short years ago had lost its appeal. It was empty.

Meaningless.

God used the scene to speak into my soul. *Here is the kind of work I do* (referencing the sunset), *and that* (referencing the parking lot full of empty lives) *is all you have. Wouldn't you rather be a part of My kind of work—and the life I can give?* The words weren't audible, but I knew they were true and they were for me.

At the end of the road there was a T intersection. To turn right would have meant more of the same—which I no longer wanted. To turn left meant taking the road back home—the road to a new start, the road to a God kind of life. I wasn't sure what it would mean or what it would look like. But wherever this path would take me had to better than what I had known thus far.

I turned left . . .

My soul was awakened . . .

There is life after the yellow ragged couch!

A BRIDGE TO BUILD

AWAKEN

Every man who knocks on the door of a brothel is looking for God . . . . —G. K Chesterton

What is fun? On the surface it is a simple question. Maybe even an innocent one. But it reveals something significant.

Let's imagine that it is Thursday. It has already been a long week. You are sitting at lunch with a few of your friends, and someone says, "Let's do something fun this weekend!" What are the images that come to mind? What are the activities that people suggest? What would you look forward to doing?

How you answer that question says something important about the health of your soul. Plato said, "One can discover more about a person in an hour of play than in a year of conversation."

So I don't ask the question cynically. It is important. Perhaps more important than we think. What we do is always a reflection of who we are. What we do for fun moves us beyond our formally defined roles and gives us a chance to live without our masks for a while. Therefore, our fun preferences say something substantial about who we are at the core—about our soul.

So let me ask you to consider that question more seriously: What is fun for you?

There is a saying, out of the Old Testament of the Bible, written by one whom some consider to be the wisest man to have ever lived on Planet Earth, King Solomon. *The Message* captures the saying like this:

> *There's a way of life that looks harmless enough; look again—it leads straight to hell. Sure, those people appear to be having a good time, but all that laughter will end in heartbreak.* Proverbs 14:12–13

Maybe this reminds you of the worst sermon you ever heard. Maybe it involved a man who liked shouting, sweating, and spitting. Maybe you picked up the impression that God is anti-fun, and if you even thought about having a good time you'd be in trouble—and yes, on your way to hell!

But hang with me for a moment.

Going back to the original language, the passage actually speaks of a kind of life where there is "no life." As a result, other translations capture the saying this way:

> *There is a way that seems right to a man, but in the end it leads to death.* (NIV)

Could it be that the writer is suggesting that there is a kind of life that seems fun to the world at large, but in reality there is no life there after all? Perhaps that lack of life simply extends into eternity. Could it be that this pronouncement is not a fun-free edict from on high? Is Solomon simply giving voice to the things that many of us already know? Maybe . . . it's *not* actually about the arbitrary rules that God, the Church, or moms and dads devise. Perhaps the point is that there are certain activities, values, and lifestyles that are universally unsatisfying, simply because they can never ultimately give life to the soul—and the soul is longing to evolve.

Maybe it really is true that some people appear to be having a good time, but all the laughter invariably leads to heartbreak. Do you ever feel that way? I did for a long time, I was just afraid to admit it. I didn't really want to see it.

Looking in the Mirror

I grew up in a home with great parents. We had our own set of challenges (like every family), but my folks got most things right. I am grateful for their love, guidance, and example. They lived life well. One of the lessons my parents worked hard at teaching me was that *being good* was the best way to do life. Be honest. Work hard. Go to church. Love people. Be good. This is how life is best lived.

The problem for me growing up, listening to that message, was that being good wasn't really fun. It wasn't cool. In fact, the more I tried to be good, the more out-of-sync I felt with everyone else.

We attended a church that had some clear descriptions of what it meant to be good. Obey the rules: don't smoke, lie, cheat, or hang with those who do. My parents were religious people, so our family followed the rules. One of these rules was that no one was allowed to do any work on Sunday. It was a rule based on one of the Ten Commandments about keeping the Sabbath holy. In practice, what that meant for me was that I wasn't allowed to play baseball on Sunday.

When I was about ten, I played ball for a team that was actually pretty decent. We were in the playoffs, but unfortunately the first playoff game was rained out. The makeup game was scheduled for, yep, you guessed it . . . Sunday afternoon.

Oh no, not Sunday!

When the coach told me about the makeup game, I immediately began developing a strategy to convince my parents that there should be an exception to the no-baseball-on-Sunday rule. Baseball wasn't really work. It was fun! People ought to have fun on Sunday. If God was interested in people being on the side of good, then He most certainly ought to allow kids to play baseball on Sunday. Right?

My compelling speech didn't work. I gave it my best shot, but there was no convincing my parents otherwise. God's ways are not our ways. Rules are meant to be followed—even when they are hard. Blah, blah, blah . . .

On playoff Sunday, I got into the car in silence. I had dressed in silence. I had eaten breakfast in silence. I sulked all the way to church. I didn't talk in my Sunday school class. During the church service, I sat at the end of the pew, as far away as possible from my parents. Nothing could have felt more unfair. I loved baseball, and not being allowed to play on Sunday seemed like the most stupid rule of all.

Being good is no fun!

After church, we had coffee hour in the fellowship hall. I took three cookies. I was only supposed to take one, but I was tired of silly rules. Breaking the rules was more fun.

When I got back into the car to go home, I was still pouting. Once we were on the highway, my dad cleared his throat. He always cleared his throat when he was about to say something important. He said, "Piet, your mom and I were thinking about your game today. We have decided that we are going to let you play. People should be able to have fun on Sunday. Playing baseball is fun for you, and you are good at it. We're going to let you play."

I could not have been happier. I threw my arms around my dad's neck. I think I almost caused an accident. I was elated. I felt guilty about the cookies, but nothing would steal my joy.

When I got home, I rushed upstairs to change into my uniform. I stuffed down a ham sandwich. Still eating, I hopped onto my bicycle and pedaled furiously. I was going to be a couple minutes late, but surely the coach would understand.

When I got to the field, I was riding up the sideline. I caught the coach's eye. He was not happy. He looked the other way. I was late. The game had already started. When I put down my bike and headed over to the bench, the coach turned and caught me by the arm. "*Where do you think you're going, kid?*" he said. I stammered. I tried to explain about church and Sunday. He wasn't interested.

He said, "You know the rules. You're late, you don't play! You're riding the bench today, son . . ."

Seriously?

Now it became inarguable. Trying to be good is no fun at all!

In eighth grade they showed us a video of the dangers of drugs and alcohol. It was stupid. Everyone poked fun of it afterward. It was a little extreme and overdone. Mostly, it was not helpful in encouraging goodness.

If you asked any of the kids I knew in high school the question: What is fun? we had a one-word answer: *Party!* That one word said it all, but it meant many things. It meant hanging out. It meant getting high. It meant making out. It meant listening to music and talking about bands. It meant going to concerts and doing acid. It meant camping out and drinking beer. It meant living like you wanted. No rules! That was fun. That *is* fun!

Looking back on what happened, I'd be lying if I said I didn't have any fun in those days. I had moments when I experienced pleasurable feelings. I laughed. I felt part of the crowd. I was cool.

But it wasn't enough.

I remember on many occasions coming home after partying and thinking to myself, *Is this all there is? Is this what the fuss is all about?* But I never talked about it. I thought a lot about it, just never said anything about it. Reflecting on it now, I believe we all felt it at some level. But we just went along, because this was how we defined *fun.* This was how everyone defined it. There was no arguing with it. Anyone who questioned the party scene was just weird. So we just kept having fun. Fun! Was that what we were having? Yeah, that's right. *This* is fun! Or so I kept trying to convince myself.

I believe that every spiritual journey begins with an awakening. It begins with a moment of clarity. It begins with a realization that what I know now is not enough. What I think I have is not enough. What I have experienced to date is not enough. There is something more—something more out there! I want to know it. I want to see it. I want to experience it.

In my view, this is what it feels like to begin to have your soul awakened. It is a sense of unsettledness. It is uncomfortable. It is *not* fun. But paying attention to that sensation may help one discover the truth about fun—along with many other important matters.

Could someone be praying for your unsettledness?

So long as a person thinks that what they know and experience is enough for them, they have no reason to look for more. If what they are doing for fun is still fun for them, they have no motivation to change. They have no reason to seek something more or to be something different. What they have is enough. Therefore, no amount of preaching, arguing, or threatening will change their point of view.

When I was at my worst place spiritually, I had a girlfriend who was very concerned about where I was headed. I was getting high pretty much every day. I was dealing drugs and skipping classes. I was a mess, and she knew it!

She thought an evangelistic crusade might help. She threatened to tell my parents about my drug usage if I didn't go with her to hear the evangelist. So I went with her to hear David Wilkerson at Madison Square Garden. I got high before I went. I didn't listen. I excused my own rebellion by railing against the hypocrisy of the others who attended. I was also convinced the meeting was really just about the money. I didn't "get saved" that night. A week afterward, Cindy told my parents about what I'd been doing. But even my parents' deep disappointment and grief didn't change my attitude. I was still having fun and still liked my life. I had yet to see the truth.

But then there came a day.

For me, it was sitting on a ragged yellow couch with my best friend, Chuck, after a party that went way too long and created way too big a mess. It came after my friend proudly proclaimed that he was at the beginning of his venture into the party scene, while I was ready to proclaim that I was done with mine. I saw something was missing. That is really the only thing I can take credit for. I was willing to see the disheartening truth about my life. I looked at it—

and named it. *This* was not enough. It was time to seek something new and different.

It was a long process that ended with a kind of internal declaration of intent.

I am not even sure I would have called myself a *spiritual seeker* when I first felt things shifting inside. But what I did know was that things needed to change. What I was doing wasn't working. The information I had wasn't helping. The life I was leading wasn't what I wanted. I needed something different, and for the first time in my life I became aware that what I needed wasn't in me. I became open to something outside myself. I wasn't sure what. I was pretty sure it wasn't what I grew up around, but then again, maybe it was. I just wasn't sure. All I knew was that I was asking life-shaping questions proactively for the first time in my life.

But this isn't just about me and my story; I am also hoping to build a bridge to you and your story.

The truth, of course, is that I don't know you, and you are just beginning to get to know me. We are just beginning to relate—and most relationships progress slowly, because trust comes slowly. That said, I feel compelled to say something bold. It could feel a bit premature. However, I always (okay, almost always) appreciate it when people are open and direct with me. If someone has something they really want to say, I'd rather they just say it, as opposed to hinting at it in hopes that I will somehow pick it up along the way.

I want to take that kind of risk with you.

I really don't believe in accidents. You picked up this book for a reason, or someone gave it to you thinking it might be of help to you. I suspect they care about you, and though this may sound a bit presumptuous, I care for you as well.

If that isn't odd enough, let me take it one step further. I believe God helped me to write this book for you. I certainly don't mean to suggest that I have it all figured out. However, I say this because I believe it is important for me to be open about what happened in the process of writing this manuscript.

I am an average person. I barely graduated high school. I have made my share of mistakes. In fact, I am far from perfect.

The point is that as you read through these pages, you might find yourself thinking things like, *This guy is saying things that make sense; he is putting words to what is going on in my head; apparently he must know a lot about people . . .* I don't think that's it. I am amazingly ordinary. You can even ask my wife.

However, if we can concede—or even begin to imagine—that something spiritual is active in the universe, if we can assume that such an entity exists and that this deity probably cares about creation and humanity in particular, then it is perhaps also conceivable that God just might take a very ordinary man's story and use it for good in the lives of others. He might just be active enough to make sure this book found its way into your hands, in much the same way that he spoke to me through the scene I saw at Seaside Park.

So if you start to feel understood, or if my story reminds you of yours, or if you think this really might be meant *for* you—then perhaps God is the One who is drawing you to himself. Maybe He is at work prompting your soul to life.

Perhaps this is where you would expect someone like me to talk about how short our time on earth really is, and that it's time to get these things sorted out—sooner rather than later. Perhaps you think I will now mention that you never know when a bus might veer out of control and run you over . . . Ummm, by the way, you might watch out for the one to your left, the driver looks a bit shaky . . . Too much caffeine, I suspect . . .

Nice evade! But back to the point.

The truth is that these are important matters. You already know that or you wouldn't be reading these words. Important matters can't be settled quickly or haphazardly. They deserve careful consideration. So I'm not asking you for a snap decision. I'm not even asking that you agree with everything I write. Instead, what I'd ask of you is that you remain open. Don't dismiss the questions that may be forming inside you.

Is it possible that God is actually trying to get my attention?

Is it possible that the things I think I know about spiritual matters are not yet complete?

Is it possible that my soul is longing to evolve?

Is there something here for me?

Looking to the Sky

Not surprisingly perhaps, people's hesitation in responding to an invitation from God is not unlike how they respond to other kinds of relational commitments.

My wife and I mentor and counsel couples who want to get married. We have been doing so for more than twenty years. There is a difference between talking to a couple who has been previously married and those who are getting married for the first time.

Couples who have been married before tend to be less idealistic about marriage. They are often suspicious and skeptical about lifelong relationships. Trust comes more slowly. Can you blame them? They have failed and been failed. There are few things in life that are more heart-wrenching than going through a divorce. Therefore, looking at marriage as a viable relational option (after a divorce) doesn't come easy. There is a lot to get over.

Talking to people about the Christian faith in our day is a lot like talking to divorcees about marriage. The Christian faith has been around for a while. Our history is not stellar. Christian leaders have disappointed us. Christian institutions have failed us. We are suspicious and skeptical. Trust comes slowly.

Yet in the same way that a divorce does not negate the good that is possible in a future marriage, perhaps the same thing can be said about God and the Christian faith. Perhaps, amidst the disappointments and betrayals people have experienced around church and with God, there is still something of value to be explored and known.

I have good friends who have experienced truly tragic things around the Church—from the more extreme experiences of sexual abuse to the more common experiences of broken trust and relational disappointments. In talking with them about their healing and restoration they each mention an important distinction that was critical to their progress. They had to come to the realization that people are not God. Even people who claim to represent God are not God. Even people whom God uses to do amazing things for good are not God.

Only God is God.

That sounds so obvious. But it isn't. I have watched so many people get sidetracked in their spiritual journey because of their inability to make this simple but essential distinction.

I am not suggesting that there is anything less horrific about some of the sins that hypocritical Christians and unethical Church leaders have committed against others. I am not attempting to excuse or minimize the tragedies—especially if you yourself are a victim. These things *are* tragic. They are reprehensible. People deserve better. You deserved better. The point is simply that God did not do these things to you—people did. We can have the discussion at some point on how a supposedly all-powerful God can allow such tragedies to occur—and whether or not He is guilty simply by association—but for the moment let me invite you to keep those matters separate.

Let's give God a chance to speak for himself. Wouldn't you want that same thing if people were trying to get to know you?

People can hear about you from others. People can gain certain impressions about you through the people who say they know you well. People can learn a lot about you by knowing your family. But if someone really wants to know you, the real you, then they ought to talk to you. They ought to learn about you from you. They ought to spend some time with you. Don't you hate being pre-judged by others before they have even taken the time to get to know you? It is so unfair. How can people write you off before they even know you? It is hurtful. It isn't right.

But consider this: Don't people often do that very thing with God?

We make judgments about Him, because of what people (who say they know Him) have done. We watch how they act when it comes to processing a particular political issue, or what they say about morality, or even how they act among themselves, arguing about things that really don't seem to matter at all. Then we say, "Well, if that is what God is like, I'm not interested!" Wait a minute. That wasn't God. That was people.

In thinking about what it means to be a spiritual seeker, I am suggesting that one looks for God by looking *to* God.

Talk to God about these matters. Extend to God the same courtesy you expect from others. Go directly to Him. Ask God to reveal himself. Be open enough to see Him as He is, on His own merits.

If this is where you find yourself, let that journey begin in earnest!

May I suggest a prayer that you could make your own?

O God, this feels strange trying to formulate words to describe where I am and to attempt to open myself up to You. There is a sense in which this doesn't really even feel like me. The truth is, I am not even sure if You exist. But I am at a place where I need more than what I have. I will admit I have my issues as they relate to You and what You are like. I have lots of questions, both personal and philosophical. I'm not sure how all that is going to get sorted out, but I agree that it is only fair that I give You a shot to meet with me. It seems reasonable to offer You a chance to speak for yourself. I will concede that I am not sure what to expect and how all this works. So I am going to trust more in Your ability to get through to me than in my ability to hear from You.

YOUR STORY

SEARCH

Marilyn Monroe said someone once told her she had a good soul, but she could never find it.

Our desire for happiness is the fuel behind our soul's ultimate pursuit. Fun has appeal in any given life moment, but to know true happiness is the aim of life. So let me ask you a one-step-deeper kind of question. What will make you happy? Take a moment to think about this. Don't self-edit. Be honest.

Is it money? Do you believe that more money would make you happier? Sometimes people have trouble being honest with themselves about this. They don't like admitting that some of their desires seem materialistic or selfish. But if this process is going to have value, you have to be honest about what is really happening inside.

So ponder it for a while. Don't push past it too quickly. I appreciate a statement I once heard Ruth Haley Barton share at a spiritual retreat I attended: "The questions we are asking are more important than the answers we think we know."

So if you are wondering whether or not money will make you happy, stop and sit with that question for a while. Some people want to argue that money is not their focus. They are deeper than that. However, it is still possible to assume (even subconsciously) that having *more* financial resources (and the security and the stuff it provides) would actually make one happier. It's okay to admit that. So let me ask it again: *Will more money make you happier?*

I suspect you are familiar with the surveys that have been conducted on the connection between money and happiness. Oddly enough, there is *no* verifiable cause and effect relationship between money in the bank and levels of personal happiness. Members of the Forbes 400 list are statistically no happier than the Maasi herdsmen of East Africa.

Money can't buy you happiness! Your grandmother was right after all. But perhaps you'd still like to be a test case. The thought certainly crosses my mind periodically. But, truthfully, haven't you already tried that? Haven't we all tried that?

When I was in third grade I broke my elbow. I was riding my brother's bike and hit an icy patch, thus destroying the bike. My mom was giving me grief about taking my brother's bike without permission—until she saw the bone sticking out of my arm. Then she put the lecture on hold in order to take me to the emergency room.

Over the Christmas holiday I was confined to bed, and my parents had pity on me. That year, I begged and pleaded for a particular toy, one I had seen advertised on TV. It included a car jumping through a cardboard hoop of flames. It was so cool! I wanted it so bad. My parents weren't inclined to give in to my materialistic pleadings, but that year was different. I was in bed. I was in a cast. I was well-positioned to get exactly what I wanted and that year I did.

But, as all kids learn, the things that I thought would buy me happiness didn't. The toy car was broken by February. The cardboard flames didn't look as good in reality as they did on TV. Sometimes the car didn't even stay on the track. In fact, after a couple of times seeing it go through the hoop, I thought, *What's the point?* I got bored with it.

I can say the same thing about every car I bought, every computer system I purchased, every vacation I ever went on, and every motorcycle I ever owned. Okay, maybe the motorcycle was a bit different. I loved my fiftieth-anniversary Daytona Edition Harley Davidson, but I crashed it, too—proving once again that even the things that "do it" for you don't last. Jesus said that the stuff that many of us spend our lives pursuing, rust out, wear out, and burn out. So it makes sense, doesn't it, to invest our lives in the things that go beyond the material realm?

Perhaps you *have* moved beyond the stuff. Maybe your hope for happiness comes in the form of a relationship. Maybe you can honestly say that you aren't materialistic. You know there is no sustaining appeal in that arena for you. Maybe you have even watched other people wreck their lives in the pursuit of it, and you don't want to repeat their mistakes. So you get it.

Therefore, as you ponder this question, you might say that your happiness is tied into having a relationship that leads to marriage—or a deep and meaningful relationship of any kind. You are tired of being lonely. You'd love to share life with someone who loves you and values you. You see other people who have a spouse they enjoy, someone to do activities with, someone to talk to, and you don't have anyone. So, you reason, if you could find someone, and get married, then you would be happy.

Early in my career, I spent a lot of time with college students. We often had students in our home. I can remember literally dozens of conversations with students who were lamenting the fact that they would probably never get married. Sometimes they had just walked through a really hard break-up, or maybe they hadn't been on a date for months (maybe even years). They were so distraught and felt so alone. They would sit at our kitchen table, an absolute mess, melancholy about the prospects of being single for the rest of their lives. It sounds dramatic, but their feelings were real. I would try to reassure them that they still had so much of their lives ahead of them—that at twenty-one years of age there were still a host of options available and time enough to discover them.

I am happy to report that every person I talked to over our kitchen table ended up finding someone and getting married. I have kept in touch with a few of them. Isn't Facebook great?

Even so, guess what? The best of these marriages experience hardship and trouble. Some have even ended in divorce. Each of these formally distraught college students who were pleading with God to find someone special have discovered that finding the "right one" does not guarantee happiness. True life-sustaining happiness requires something more—something deeper!

The fact is that sustained happiness is elusive. It isn't found in the stuff of this life. It isn't guaranteed through great relationships. In fact, we could go on and reference a host of other sources that people have explored in the hopes of finding lasting happiness— drugs/alcohol, adrenaline-driven experiences, pleasure, power, good works, religion, etc. In the end, the story always sounds the same. In the words of Bono, many of us say, "I still haven't found what I am looking for . . ."

If that is true, if everything we have tried leaves us wanting more, then we are left to draw one of two conclusions: Either real happiness isn't possible and therefore we ought to give up trying to experience it at all; or we have to consider looking for it in places that people don't traditionally go to find it.

Many have concluded that finding sustained happiness just isn't possible. Perhaps that is what is at the heart of the Epicurean philosophy, which states, "Eat, drink, and be merry for tomorrow we die!" However, many of us have already been there—and found no real relief either—which brings us to option two. Maybe sustainable joy is found in the places we don't typically look for it. Perhaps it *is* spiritual in nature. But if it is, that presents an interesting dilemma in itself, because the discovery of spiritual reality is not an exact science.

We live our lives in a physical realm—typically dealing with the things we can taste, touch, see, hear, and smell. Therefore, discovering spiritual truth is not something that comes *naturally*. We may sense things. We may have certain impressions and ideas that we pick up on along the way. But most of us feel ill-suited for this kind of spiritual exploration process. We are not sure what spiritual seeking really entails. If this is the path to real happiness, it seems ominous, mysterious, and unclear. But then again, perhaps a measure of humility is a good thing at this point. We probably ought not underestimate the energy and effort involved.

That said, my purpose is to try to keep things simple. I want to use normal words. I want to describe a process that anyone from any background can understand and take action on. Regrettably, there aren't many Christian authors who are very good at that—at least in my experience. I think all too often we make things complicated. We tend to be more concerned about sounding smart than about being helpful. So we often make things more difficult than they need to be. As much as possible, I want to try to cut through all the complexities and all the fancy vocabulary and make this process accessible. That doesn't mean it will be easy to do, but it ought to at least be easy to understand!

Here is what I have discovered. Our search for sustained happiness (spiritually) is most likely to be successful when we engage the journey *proactively.*

On the surface that might not sound difficult. Many people believe they are ready to do just that. Perhaps you feel like you are already trying to do that. But I want to suggest that in our day, and in this area particularly, it may be harder to do than we think.

Let me illustrate.

One of the great benefits of living in our world at this time is our general orientation toward customer service. As a culture we are used to people taking our comfort into account and anticipating what we need—and even what we want. We are used to people doing a lot of our thinking and working for us.

For example, when we buy a new car, upon the completion of our purchase we are handed a customer satisfaction survey. The car manufacturer will invite us to give commentary on our overall satisfaction with the product. They ask if there is anything that can be improved. We might mention that an extra cup holder would be nice, or how the seat is cold in the morning, or that our significant other likes it warmer on their side of the car. The next thing you know there are more cup holders in our vehicles. We now have heated seats and dual-zone climate-control systems.

In addition, there are marketing and research types who are out and about watching how we use stuff, while constantly asking the question: "What could make the use of this product easier or more convenient?" We live in a day when lots of people are doing their absolute best to know our needs/wants and then trying to meet them—even before we know how to talk about them.

It is a great day to be alive.

But consider this for just a moment. There may be a downside to all this need-meeting-obsessiveness—especially when it comes to our spiritual journey. Remember, we are talking about personal proactivity. In a day and age when we are used to people anticipating our needs/wants and doing a lot of the thinking for us, there aren't many places in our lives where we have to be all that proactive. There are simply not that many occasions in our day-to-day existence where we have to personally figure things out and dig at what is really true and important.

How does all this relate to our spiritual journey?

Take church attendance for example. Let's say you actually become interested in exploring spiritual truth. What would be a typical next step? In our culture there are buildings dedicated to worship experiences, where people talk about God at certain times of the week. These meetings are usually on Sunday mornings. The public is welcome. Perhaps you would decide to go to one of these meetings.

What goes on in people's minds as they leave for the event? I think we all have similar expectations. We hope the people we meet will be friendly and welcoming—but not overdone. We hope that our questions will be respected. In addition, we'd probably anticipate that there would be capable people ready to welcome and care for our kids. The building should be clean, easy to access, with plenty of parking. The seats ought to be comfortable. The speaker should be well-informed and helpful. The music meaningful. We come ready to observe and receive, and hopefully to be spiritually fed. We want the professionals to attend to our needs spiritually in the same way we expect other professionals to attend to our needs in all the other areas of our lives—at restaurants, service shops, workout facilities, movie theaters, and public schools.

I think we do this instinctively. It is how the culture responds to us in every other venue. So when we think about spiritual growth and think about the entities and people who service those needs, we have an expectation about what "they" will do for us. But is it possible that this causes us to become a tad naïve about the process? Have we brought too many of our personal preferences and assumptions about cultural norms to the spiritual investigation process? Is it reasonable for us to assume that if we just sit and listen (in an environment that has been designed to cater to our needs and wants) that someday it will all just become clear to us? Will we be changed for the better without really having to engage proactively?

Is that realistic?

On a positive note, it does seem likely that sitting through an experience and listening to a gifted teacher may enable us to see things in a new way. We may even be exposed to some ideas that we hadn't considered before. Comfortable chairs and quality sound systems do remove distractions—therefore the environment does matter.

However, thinking about this on the most basic level, I have to ask: Will the reception of helpful information in comfortable surroundings *alone* make us happier and more spiritually mature? Will this approach make spiritual truth more real to us? Will we personally experience God at a deeper level simply because we showed up? Doesn't it have to go deeper than that!?

Here is how Jesus talked about it . . . Oh wait . . .

I do understand that the nature and status of Jesus as a reliable authority figure may still be in question for you. Perhaps even the veracity of the manuscripts, which include His teachings, may be suspect, but for the moment let's consider the words at face value.

It was my experience that part of what convinced me that the words of Jesus had merit was that they continually "resonated" in the world in which I lived. His teaching often seemed initially counterintuitive but eventually meaningful and inspired. The more I thought about it, there was something inside of me that needed what He taught. Therefore, it is possible that giving yourself permission to consider these wisdom sayings "as though they were true" (even if you can't buy the whole deal) can by itself be a great faith-building experience.

So here is what Jesus said:

Keep on asking, and you will receive what you ask for. Keep on seeking, and you will find. Keep on knocking, and the door will be opened to you. For everyone who asks, receives. Everyone who seeks, finds. And to everyone who knocks, the door will be opened. Matthew 7:7–8, NLT

At first glance, you might be tempted to discount the validity of the promise made in this passage, because you can think of a host of things you have asked for (perhaps with great persistence) that you have never received. In addition, there are many things you have probably lost that you have never recovered (keys, credit cards, or time spent at the DMV). And talk about closed doors! If you have ever been in the sales profession, you have probably had your fair share of doors slammed in your face. So the whole thrust of the statement doesn't strike us as true at all. It actually seems too good to be true.

But is it possible that there is a deeper meaning behind the words?

This statement is actually part of an extended teaching that covers three chapters in the Gospel of Matthew (beginning in Matthew chapter 5). It is a part of what is usually referred to as Jesus' Sermon on the Mount, and what Jesus is talking about in this sermon is the nature of the life that He has come to initiate—or what He refers to as life in the Kingdom of God.

In other words, Jesus was describing a new kind of life, a life where God is at the center and where His love and truth rule the day. In this talk, Jesus was describing what this spiritually motivated life looks like, feels like, acts like—and toward the end of His speech He starts talking about how one can gain access to this kind of life!

It is almost as though Jesus is anticipating the question the crowd might ask next. He is wrapping up His talk on all these grand ideals of a God-centered, God-valued, God-motivated way of doing life, and He can imagine people getting excited about the prospects of it and then asking the question, "How do we tap in to that kind of life?"

He anticipates their question, and He gives them this answer: *You gotta seek it out.*

You gotta ask!

You gotta knock!

What I find especially helpful about the translation I quoted is that it gives us a hint of the verb tense in the original language. It is written in the present continuous tense. So Jesus is saying: Ask and *keep on* asking. Seek, and *keep on* seeking. Knock, and *keep on* knocking. There is all this good available, but you're going to have to go after it with a fully engaged soul.

Be proactive!

With that, let me hit the PAUSE button for a moment.

I have had this kind of conversation with many people—from all walks of life. It is not uncommon for them to agree with the gist of what I have described thus far. They are hungry for more. They haven't discovered that ultimate sense of fulfillment yet. They realize that what they have known to date isn't enough. They want to be happy, but happiness is elusive. Perhaps you are willing to admit some of these same things. But you're not sure what that means. You are ready to be diligent, but you want to know where to begin. Perhaps you find yourself wondering, *How do I seek . . . knock . . . ask? Ask who what? Seek what where? Knock on which door?*

Satisfying the Curiosity of the Mind

One of the things I have noticed as I have tried to be of help to people along this path is that different people face different kinds of belief challenges. For some people the greatest challenge to spiritual progress is related to what is happening in their minds.

Their fundamental challenge is intellectual in nature.

They have questions about the validity and integrity of the facts. They may want to believe in God, but they can't get past the problem of evil, or how we can know for sure that what is written in books like the Bible is, in fact, trustworthy. They may have good feelings in the context of certain meetings and worship experiences, but they don't want to base their faith commitments on feelings alone. They are often envious about the ease at which some people come to believe, and yet they find themselves stuck on matters of science, ethics, and philosophy.

These are important questions, and there ought to be no shame in wanting to take them seriously. Perhaps this is your primary hurdle. If so, then this is the arena in which you would want to be the most proactive. Navigate the biggest hurdle first.

A word of caution, however.

Sometimes people use their intellectual questions as a reason not to have to change their point of view. The questions are actually a smokescreen. The unanswerable questions legitimize a lifestyle they are not ready to change. I did that. Respect yourself enough not to play games. If you're not ready—you're not ready. Remember, the unsettledness must come first.

However, if a person is genuinely curious about the intellectual issues that are raised about the Christian faith, there are some very smart people who have written some extremely helpful books that are worthy of your proactive engagement. Let me suggest a few:

Mere Christianity by C. S. Lewis

Evidence That Demands a Verdict by Josh McDowell

The Case for Christ by Lee Strobel

Letters from a Skeptic by Greg Boyd

Velvet Elvis by Rob Bell

These are great resources, and these authors do a great job of wrestling through the weightier matters of our faith. In fact, if this is the area where you face your greater challenges, consider picking up one of these resources and use it as a companion guide to the work you are doing here.

Satisfying the Longings of Your Heart

For others the primary issue is a matter of the heart. They have knowledge *about* God; they just don't have an experience *with* Him.

A doctor friend of mine started attending church, primarily because his wife bugged him to go. Over the course of time, we got to know each other a bit. I had started a skeptics' small group where I met over lunch (once a month) with three guys who were having a really hard time with some of the specifics of Christian doctrine. I invited this doctor friend to join us.

Over the course of the next six to nine months, we went through some of the books noted above, and my friend started getting some of his questions answered. After one of our lunch meetings, he pulled me aside and said, "You know, I think I have most of the intellectual issues resolved, at least I am not put off in the same way I was before." Then he said, "I think what I really need now is an experience. I need to feel God. I have never had an experience where I can say that God was real to me. I hear people talk about how they sense God's presence or God's comfort, but I have never felt that. And if I am ever going to move toward devotion to God, I think I need something like that."

I was excited for him, because I know God loves revealing himself to us.

If you search for him with all your heart and soul, you will find him. Deuteronomy 4:29, NLT

Notice that the promise is given without equivocation. If we seek Him—we will find Him. The only qualifier is that we be willing to engage in an all-out search, a search worthy of the soul.

I am afraid that many people who desire an experience with God don't really want to give Him enough time or space to reveal himself, or they have predetermined what God needs to do in order to be convinced. But isn't the point that God shows himself to us as He is? We need God himself, not some prepackaged version of a god we make up in our minds.

Yet we live in an automated society where we are used to things happening quickly and easily. We live in a day and time where marketing slogans affirm our right to have it *our* way. Therefore, it requires no small internal adjustment for us to honestly search for God and to give Him the time He needs to reveal himself in the way He desires. The good news is that He will, should we give Him the time and freedom to do so, engaging our soul in a way that reflects the importance of the task.

So when my friend told me about his desire for an experience, I encouraged him to start praying a simple prayer, sincerely, on a regular basis:

God, open my eyes, I want to see You. I want to feel You. I want to know You.

I invited him to begin expecting God to answer that prayer. I also encouraged him to schedule an extended time where he could sit and wait for God to reveal himself.

I don't remember exactly how long it was before I got the call back from him, but my friend took a trip to give a lecture in Boston. After he gave the lecture, he had some unexpected downtime. He decided to walk in the downtown area. It was a beautiful spring day. He noticed a cathedral where the doors were open. He walked inside. He took a seat, and he came back to that little prayer I had encouraged him to pray: *"God, open my eyes, I want to see You. I want to feel You. I want to know You."*

As he sat there he noticed a crucifix on the wall, and he was taken by the image. He started remembering the things he had been reading about, and he sat there for about an hour. In that time and space, where he slowed down long enough to give God room, he experienced a kind of joy that went deeper than anything he had ever experienced before. His soul evolved. His heart was given verification of the things that his mind had begun to believe.

It was that simple. Yet it took that long.

Dear God, Friend of the seeker, would You provide multiple signals of Your reality to the one reading here? Surprise them. Meet them. Let them meet You in a way that satisfies both their heart and mind.

DOUBT

There is a difference between knowing the path and walking the path . . . —Morpheus

He is the poster child for Doubters Anonymous. For the last two thousand years or so, if anyone had trouble believing something, they were admonished not to be a "Doubting Thomas." The admonition is typically given with a snarl and a condescending look. What is clear is that no one should ever be *that*.

Thomas is actually one of my heroes. I think he has gotten a bad rap. In fact, I believe there is a lot that we can learn from him. We read about Thomas's story in John 20.

Thomas was one of the twelve disciples of Jesus—meaning essentially that he was one of the leaders of the group. He had been with Jesus from the beginning. He was a true believer. After Jesus had been crucified, He arose from the dead and appeared to His disciples, at various times and places. One of the initial appearances was at a meeting that Thomas missed. When he was told about what happened, he was, well . . . a bit skeptical. He doubted the report.

But Thomas, sometimes called the Twin, one of the Twelve, was not with them when Jesus came. The other disciples told him, "We saw the Master." But he said, "Unless I see the nail holes in his hands, put my finger in the nail holes, and stick my hand in his side, I won't believe it." Eight days later, his disciples were again in the room. This time Thomas was with them. Jesus came through the locked doors, stood among them, and said, "Peace to you." Then he focused his attention on Thomas. "Take your finger and examine my hands. Take your hand and stick it into my side. Don't be unbelieving. Believe." Thomas said, "My Master! My God!"
John 20:24–28, MSG

Put yourself in Thomas's place for a moment. Maybe that is not hard to do. Perhaps that's where you live. It's possible that you feel badly about this—especially around people who seem so self-assured and full of faith. But the fact is, you are in good company.

Let's take another look at the story of Thomas.

Thomas, like all the disciples, had put his complete hope and trust in Jesus' teaching. He altered his life to center around the One who came to be called the Christ. However, we also have enough information about Thomas to know that he was able to speak his mind and ask penetrating and uncomfortable questions. Doubt and faith seemed to live together inside this man. Even so, Jesus chose him. He was a leader in the movement.

After being with Jesus day in and day out for three years, Thomas came to believe that Jesus was the promised Messiah. Like the others, Thomas gave up his own hopes and dreams and pinned them totally on Jesus and His mission on the earth. He took a huge risk for Jesus. He wasn't just one of those casual observers who hid his admiration out of fear of the other religious leaders. He was totally *in*. He had declared his faith!

He wasn't one of these waffling followers who would praise Jesus on Palm Sunday only to turn on Him when He was accused and sentenced before Pilate. Thomas was there to the end. He had watched His Master die—and with Him, all of Thomas's dreams died as well. Thomas was crushed. He was devastated. Everything he had put his hope in had turned out to be a lie—or so it seemed.

Is it possible that the reason Thomas missed the meeting (where Jesus made His first appearance) was because he was still grieving—perhaps at a deeper level—than some of the others? He just couldn't bring himself to show up. He didn't want them to see his tears. Have you ever been in that same kind of place where you have been so hurt, so confused, so upended that it was hard for you to even be around people?

I feel quite sure that this is where Thomas was. He had been deeply disappointed by life and by God. He believed. He followed. He put his trust in something that he thought would make the world a better place, and it was all snuffed out—just like that! Gone! Crucified! Over! Finished!

Then, in a matter of days, Thomas heard that it might not be over after all. There was new information. The mission was not yet over. Jesus was alive! When that news reached Thomas, he uttered his infamous words:

"Unless I see the nail holes in his hands, put my finger in the nail holes, and stick my hand in his side, I won't believe it."

It is these words that earn him the title "Doubting Thomas." Is that a fair indictment? Thomas asks for confirming evidence. Should that make him the prince of doubters? Sometimes when we read an account in a purported "holy book," we can find it difficult to imagine ourselves in the story. But if we can use our imagination and put ourselves there, it brings the story to life.

So imagine yourself there for a moment.

When you have really given yourself to something and it doesn't turn out like you expect, isn't it natural and normal to be a little more cautious the next time around? We actually assume people are a bit unstable when they are too quick to recommit to something that has just cost them everything. We wonder about their emotional stability if they are too quick to believe again.

So let me be candid. The more I think about Thomas, the more heroic he becomes, because at least Thomas knew what he needed to make a comeback, and he was willing to declare that.

Notice that he didn't say, "You know what, I am tired, I am burned out, I have given my heart away for the last time. I don't care what you say; there is nothing that God could do that will change my mind. I am not going to put myself out there again." He didn't say that! He could have—but he didn't! It wouldn't take us long to think of names and faces of people who end up in that place. Maybe you are tempted to be one yourself.

For some, the disappointment with life and God runs so deep and the sense of betrayal feels so core, they just turn it totally off. Faith feels beyond them. But what does Thomas do? He says, in effect, *I am still willing to believe, but I just need some evidence. Here is what I think I need.* Then he declares it.

One of the highlights of the story for me is that Jesus accommodates that request, and my sense is that He does so willingly and graciously. As I read this text and try to imagine the manner in which Jesus does what He does—when He sees Thomas for the first time—I sense nothing but love and mercy coming from Him. He says, in effect, "Thomas, I have heard your cry. Here are My hands. Here is My side . . . If this helps you get what you need, I am willing and ready to give that to you."

Interestingly, after the encounter, Jesus makes the comment that not everyone will get to see the nail-pierced hands, and not everyone will get to stick their hand in the side that was pierced with a sword. Therefore Jesus said, "Blessed are those who believe though without seeing me" (John 20:29, NLT).

This statement is not an indictment of Thomas. I think Jesus loved Thomas deeply! Rather His statement is an affirmation of those who have chosen to believe even without being given the opportunity to see what Thomas saw. It is an encouragement to all who, in the midst of their questions and doubts, are still able to express and maintain even just a shred of belief in their soul.

What Is God Asking of You?

Summarizations of God's purposes are risky business. Albert Haase said it well: "Human language always stammers, limps and collapses when trying to express or communicate the wisdom of God. Whatever is said or written about God will be off mark and prone to misunderstanding and error."

Eckhard adds: "The hand that writes the true thing about God is the hand that erases."

So I proceed cautiously.

However, I believe this much can be said with confidence: God is anxious to be known by you and to be central in your life's story. I believe that the willingness of Jesus to give Thomas what he needed is reflective of God's heart toward all of us. Therefore, I believe that the Spirit of God is already active in your soul—perhaps even in ways that you are not aware of yet—where He is drawing you to himself.

I have spoken to all kinds of people for over thirty years about what it means to have a meaningful and personal connection to God. At the risk of oversimplifying, the issue that most people find unsettling is the relevance and necessity of it all.

I find people wondering why God matters. It is not so much that people are vehemently anti-God—although I have met a few who are—and sometimes their vehement denials are actually a signal that they are closer to belief than we think. Their animation and demonstrative critiques are a sign that something spiritually significant is stirring deep within.

But most of the time, the issues and reactions are much more subdued. There simply aren't that many people who are shaking their fists at God. For many it seems that God is simply a non-factor. Why bother? What's the point? Who cares?

I can't help but wonder if a large part of the indifference has to do with the fact that in our modern world, many of us already have such abundance. We are reasonably self-sufficient. If we get sick, we can go to the doctor. If we don't know how to invest our money, we can go to a financial advisor. Heck, if we are having trouble with our sex life, there is even a pill that can help with that.

So why do we need God?

One of the reasons I have drawn attention to our disappointment with fun and our frustration with finding happiness is because these are the areas that most obviously reveal our hope for more. These are the places where we often feel the most unsettled. It is at these doors that the soul seems to exert its most powerful need for attention.

But what is our soul trying to find?

If the Bible has any relevance on the subject, then the longing of our soul is for God and nothing less. Our soul *knows* things that our mind and body only figure out later. That is why we label the sensation "unsettled." Our soul is speaking to us with its own language, reminding us that we need something as substantive as God to fill us—and nothing else will do. God uses these unsatisfied longings to help us find Him.

It's really a good news–bad news–good news kind of deal. The good news is that we were created as unique human beings who bear the marks of our Creator. We were made in His image. Therefore, we have significant potential. We do good. We can be good. And we can do even more good.

Unfortunately, the bad news is that though we all have potential for great good, we have chosen (each in our own way) to do our own thing. We are rebels at heart. For some the rebellion is subtle. For others it is bold. But the truth about us all is that we are inclined toward rebellious ways, rebellious thoughts, and rebellious motivations. The Bible calls this sin. It is in us—and we cannot self-repair.

But perhaps you already know this.

How many times have you given yourself to one self-improvement plan after another (to change what you thought needed improving), only to fail over and over again? This isn't just your story. This is the human story. We can change some things, but not the most important things. One of the most powerful and influential leaders of the early Church came to this very same conclusion himself. Here is how he talked about it:

But I need something more! *For if I know the law but still can't keep it, and if the power of sin within me keeps sabotaging my best intentions, I obviously need help! I realize that I don't have what it takes. I can will it, but I can't do it. I decide to do good, but I don't really do it; I decide not to do bad, but then I do it anyway. My decisions, such as they are, don't result in actions. Something has gone wrong deep within me and gets the better of me every time. It happens so regularly that it's predictable. The moment I decide to do good, sin is there to trip me up. I truly delight in God's commands, but it's pretty obvious that not all of me joins in that delight. Parts of me covertly rebel, and just when I least expect it, they take charge. I've tried everything and nothing helps. I'm at the end of my rope. Is there no one who can do anything for me? Isn't that the real question? The answer, thank God, is that Jesus Christ can and does.*
Romans 7:17–25, MSG

The good news of the message that Jesus came to deliver is that we can be made right with God, and that which has been broken inside can be healed. That is possible because something spiritually significant happened at the cross of Jesus Christ. On the surface it appears that what happened with Jesus was that a good man died unnecessarily because He was betrayed by friends who didn't understand Him and He was scandalized by religious leaders who were jealous of His influence. But in the spiritual realm, God used these tragic events and infused them with meaning that addresses our core need—forgiveness from God and the power to live a better life.

Jesus Christ took upon himself the sins of humanity. He lived an exemplary life. He taught in ways that had never been heard before. He healed the sick and did good to those who were classified as the "sinners" of His time. Even death could not keep its hold on Him. Each of these actions affirmed the unique status that Jesus alone deserves. Jesus was God wrapped in human flesh—everything we know about Him points to that. As the unique God/man, He accomplished something for us that we could never do for ourselves.

Most notably, His death and resurrection shifted something foundational in the spiritual realm, such that those who accept what happened on the cross as the sufficient covering for their sin, can know forgiveness and restoration. The soul, which has always longed to know and be made right with its Maker, is brought to life by the Spirit at the very moment that Christ's ultimate sacrifice is understood and embraced. In and through Christ, God extended grace. It is what we least deserved, but what He most longed to provide. He has made all things new.

Paul, whose personal testimony I quoted earlier, reflects on these same ideas, and even though he gave his life to communicate this truth, he, too, recognized what a hard sell this might be. So he said it straight up:

> *The Message that points to Christ on the Cross seems like sheer silliness to those hellbent on destruction, but for those on the way of salvation it makes perfect sense. This is the way God works, and most powerfully as it turns out.*
> 1 Corinthians 1:18, MSG

This is the door we are invited to knock on—and Jesus willingly opens it. Only God has the power to bring the soul to life. In Him we find ultimate soul satisfaction.

What Do You Think?

If we were having this chat over coffee, this would be the place where I'd want to pause and ask you: "What do you think about all of this?" If my conversations with others are at all reflective of what might be happening in you, I can imagine you wanting to say something close to one of three things.

One option is that you are having a hard time thinking of a way to say what you have on your mind. Maybe you would be cautious because you don't want to offend me, but then I would encourage you to be candid. So, after taking a deep breath you might say:

> Sorry, Piet, I just can't buy it. I still have too many unanswered questions. And the whole notion that something spiritually

significant happened for me, because of what happened with Jesus, is just a bit of a stretch for me. Jesus certainly said some very important things, and we'd all be better off paying attention to what He taught, but I can't go with you on that whole "He died for my sins" thing.

If that is where you find yourself, I'd say a couple things in response.

Isn't it dignifying that God gives us a choice about this? He is not going to force your hand. He gives us the option to continue attempting to self-repair. If that is the road you prefer, God gives you that freedom.

You can even set this book down. You don't have to read another page. I wouldn't even know.

But before you do, can I encourage you not to settle for the overused "Well, Jesus was at least a 'good teacher' and we'd do well to listen to what He had to say"? I do agree that Jesus was a great teacher. But He was so much more than that—and this is more than just my opinion. Jesus made some pretty outrageous claims about *himself,* claims that can't be easily sidestepped. If we believe that His teaching on morality and ethics have merit, then we probably cannot (with integrity) arbitrarily dismiss His claims regarding his identity and divinity. C. S. Lewis dealt with that issue in a compelling way:

> I am trying here to prevent anyone saying the really foolish thing that people often say about him: "I'm ready to accept Jesus as a great moral teacher, but I don't accept his claim to be God." That is the one thing we must not say.

> A man who was merely a man and said the sort of things Jesus said would not be a great moral teacher. He would either be a lunatic—on the level with the man who says he is a poached egg—or else he would be the Devil of Hell. You must make your choice.

Either this man was, and is, the Son of God, or else a madman or something worse. You can shut him up for a fool, you can spit at him and kill him as a demon or you can fall at his feet and call him Lord and God, but let us not come with any patronizing nonsense about his being a great human teacher. He has not left that open to us. He did not intend to . . . .

However, a second option is that you aren't hesitating at all.

You have been tracking from the start. These seem to be the right words at the right time. So instead of being put off by these ideas, you feel drawn in by them. Perhaps, for the first time, you find yourself ready to embrace something spiritually substantive. It isn't that you haven't ever heard or thought about these things before, but it has all resonated in a way that is fresh. You find yourself in a new place, a place where you are willing to take the big step—to give your soul permission to find what it has been longing for.

Perhaps you want to say:

Piet, I never really imagined myself saying something like this. But the truth is that this is actually all beginning to make sense to me. God's work in me began long before I picked up this book, but there is a way in which all the right things have come together for me as I have been reading this. Although it is hard to put words to everything I am feeling, I know this much: I am ready for a new start. I am ready to embrace what God has done for me in Christ. I am so tired of self-repair and so ready for grace.

If we were sitting together in a coffee shop, I would let out an enthusiastic fist-pumping "whoop"—because you are moving from death into life and from darkness into light. Hope I wouldn't have embarrassed you—but it really is that good!

One of my favorite stories out of the life of Jesus actually occurs at His darkest hour. Jesus is hanging on a cross and about to die, and there is a convicted criminal hanging next to Him on his own cross. The criminal says just a few words to Jesus before they both breathe their last breaths. He has a repentant moment and he asks to Jesus to remember him.

Remarkably, Jesus responds graciously:

"I assure you, today you will be with me in paradise."
Luke 23:43, NLT

There are several things I really appreciate about this story. First, I am amazed at the mercy and kindness of Jesus, that He would extend such selfless grace to a criminal in His own darkest hour. What love! I am also reminded that it is never too late and a person can never be too bad. But what I love most about the account is the simplicity of the conversation.

Sometimes, in Christian circles, people get very caught up with people saying the right words. Has a person said the official "sinner's prayer"? Did they get the formula right? But there are no magic words. Rather there is a disposition of the heart that moves a soul God-ward. Some of the most beautiful prayers I have ever heard are the spontaneous, unrehearsed prayers of a person who uses their own heartfelt words to give voice to what is happening inside.

Why not do that yourself, even now!

Okay, maybe you're not quite there yet.

There is a third option. It is possible (maybe even likely) that you find yourself somewhere in between. You aren't ready to close the book. But you still aren't ready to surrender yourself unreservedly to God. So our conversation might continue something like this:

Piet, there is a lot about what you are saying that makes sense to me. It rings true—in some ways. I can even say that there are days where I want to believe. But I feel stuck. I am just not sure that I can buy the whole being-a-Christian thing. There are so many expectations. It just doesn't seem like me. I don't think I'd make a very good Christian. Not very motivated. Not that good. Still enjoy things I probably shouldn't.

I respect that kind of honesty. I really do!

Let's go back to the story of Thomas for a moment. When life happened to Thomas, it was a faith-crushing experience. He wasn't sure he felt like being good or following God. However, he couldn't escape what he already knew. He couldn't escape the signs and signals that confirmed the truth about Jesus. Therefore, he just couldn't bring himself to give up completely. He knew he needed something more to get on track, and he was bold enough to ask for it.

So here is the question I would like to pose to you. It is a simple question really. It was a question that Thomas knew the answer to. The question I'd ask you to consider is: *What would it take for you to believe?* Are you willing to declare it? It is normal and natural to have doubts, but can you doubt decisively? If you can, you might be surprised at how willing God is to show you what you need.

By the way, you don't have to have everything figured out before you embrace His grace.

There is a great story in John 9, where Jesus heals a man who was born blind. The healing occurred on the Sabbath, a day of rest from all one's labors. Christ's "work" of healing was against the rules. So the religious leaders launched an investigation. When they interviewed the man who had been healed, they peppered him with various theological questions. In the end, all he could say was, "Hey guys, I really don't know how to answer your questions. All I know is that I used to be blind—and now I can see!"

When I accepted the grace made available to me through Christ, I knew that my life needed a change. I knew enough about the message of Christianity—and seen its positive effect in people I respected—such that when I came to my own crossroads, I acted on what I knew. When I walked through the door, I was changed. I knew I was different. Of course, I had questions that remained unanswered. I didn't have everything figured out. I still don't. But I knew enough to say, "Lord, would You have mercy on me—a sinner?" He did.

Lord, I continue to pray for the one reading these words. Might You graciously give exactly what is needed. Open eyes to see it. Make hearts and minds willing to explore it. And give them readiness to respond to it—as Your grace becomes clear. In Jesus' name!

RISK

The person who risks nothing, does nothing, has nothing, is nothing, and becomes nothing. He may avoid suffering and sorrow, but he simply cannot learn and feel and change and grow and love and live. —Leo F. Buscaglia

It's inevitable. Eventually a frantic call for help is made. The conversation usually sounds something like this:

"Is everything okay?"

"Yeah, I am sorry I made it sound so desperate when I called. But I have been consumed with what we have been discussing."

"Good. I'm glad . . . I think."

"I'm not really sure how to get started. It is hard to put words to all I've been thinking about. It's all so new to me. Can I just start talking, and maybe somewhere along the way I will start making some sense?"

Sure.

"Well . . . a lot of our attention has been focused on God and who He is. What He is like. What He has done. I've needed to hear that, and you have put it in a way that I can understand."

"I'm glad it has been helpful. I'm just trying to extend to you the same kindness that was shown to me."

"Well, that is actually part of it—right there—you almost make it sound like God likes me. I have heard people talk about how God loves me in a sort of obligatory altruistic sense, but you make it sound like God actually takes pleasure in me. That He isn't repulsed by my screw-ups and messy life. I am half-waiting for the hellfire and brimstone talk. I mean, isn't God upset with humanity, because of all the ways we have screwed up? Heck, isn't God upset with me? I have screwed things up!"

"And just so you have the whole story. I really don't think that I will ever get this fully straightened out. Even if I do commit my life to Christ, I am sure I am going to keep messing things up. At the end of the day, I am pretty sure I am going to let God down. I am going to let myself down. What if I don't make a very good Christian? Seriously! What if I have one beer—or five? What if I cuss? Or what if I do something a lot worse? What happens then? I'm just not sure I can do this very well . . . Not sure I will even want to."

Going All the Way There

Stop and think about the implications of Jesus coming to earth. Is it not reflective of the lengths to which God will go in order to make His love known to us? If you ponder the stories from the first portion of the Bible, what we typically refer to as the Old Testament, you can't help but notice the recurring cycle of humanity's failure and God's rescue. God offers life and extends an opportunity, but God's people are only engaged for a short while. It isn't long before they slip back into old patterns. They forget God. They act foolishly. Their consequences catch up to them. They cry out to God. He rescues them again. But very quickly, the people go back to their old ways. It happens over and over.

At a certain point, you almost expect there to be a final washing of the hands, where God says, "I am finished with you people!" That would make sense. That is what we would expect. What you don't expect is for God to move even closer. You don't expect God to wrap himself in human flesh to come to the earth to live among us, saying, "I really do want you to get this. I want you to know that I am serious about making a way for you." That is a kind of love we just can't ever totally wrap our minds around. The hymn writer said it so well, when he called this "amazing grace." It *is* amazing!

Invariably in my coffee-shop chats with spiritual seekers, the conversation will turn to some philosophizing about God's redemptive purposes for humanity. Many people can imagine that God (out of some sense of religious duty) might extend redemption to the whole of humanity more or less by fiat—from afar. It is conceivable that Christ fulfilled some legal obligation regarding the forgiveness of sins for all of humanity. If the spiritual world has some kind of legal code, and this is how God wants to administrate the system (and execute justice), that is certainly within His prerogative. They get that—they may not believe it—but they can understand it.

But it is so much more personal than that. It really is about you, too. It isn't just about humanity in some general sense; it's about you as an individual. Yes, humanity as a whole matters to God—but we would do well to remember that includes us singly and individually. *You* matter greatly to God! As Billy Graham said so often in his preaching ministry, "If you were the only person who ever lived on Planet Earth, Christ would have died for you!"

One of the most random but profound statements that Jesus ever made appears in Matthew 10. He says:

"And the very hairs on your head are all numbered."
Matthew 10:30, NLT

The comment seems to come out of left field. What an odd statement. Why would this matter? Doesn't God have more important matters to attend to? But Jesus makes this statement in the midst of a personal exhortation to His disciples, where He is (again) trying to help them understand just how much they matter to God. God will watch over them. He cannot forget them. And this is true about you as well!

What I have noticed is that for many people hearing these words (as wonderful as they are supposed to be) only remind them of their own unworthiness. They have been told that one *should* feel encouraged by these ideas, but they only compound the guilt and shame. Maybe the same is true for you.

If so, let's go back to the good news, bad news, good news idea. You'll remember that the human story begins with good news. You are God's creation. You were made by Him. You bear His image. In fact, humanity (as a whole) stands as the highlight of His created work. This is the most foundational piece of life. We were (and are) His from the beginning.

Yes, it is also true that we are flawed creatures. That's the bad news part. We haven't lived up to our potential. We aren't what we were meant to be. And yes, the bad is really bad—on the level of cosmic treason. So how does God feel about that? Is He ticked? Does the depth of our sin and rebellion put us in a place where God hates the sight of us?

The only way I know how to answer this is to think through the grid of parenting my own children. In scripture we are introduced to God as "our heavenly Father," so I believe this is a reasonable analogy to draw.

I have three children. They are each very different. They are each delightful to me. I love them deeply. I cannot imagine not loving them. No matter what! My love for them runs deeper than any disappointment I experience with them. Am I ever ticked? Of course. Have I been deeply disappointed? Yes! But whatever offense my kids committed has never erased the love. It never puts the love at risk. My love is a constant. The love is deeper—always. The good news is more foundational than the bad!

Once when Jesus was teaching about the nature of God, He built on this same analogy.

> *"Which of you, if his son asks for bread, will give him a stone? Or if he asks for a fish, will give him a snake? If you, then, though you are evil, know how to give good gifts to your children, how much more will your Father in heaven give good gifts to those who ask him!"* Matthew 7:9–11, NIV

Essentially, Jesus says, "Hey guys, you are flawed and broken people, but even you understand something of good parenting. You understand how to give good gifts to your kids. So if you in your imperfect state know how to love and bless your children, how much more so God? His love is a perfect love. You are His child! There is nothing that can erase His love for you. Yes, He even likes you!"

But maybe this hasn't answered your most pragmatic questions. What does God want from us? What am I supposed to do with this information? What if I don't do anything?

I readily admit that I don't know everything about what He is doing—no one can know that completely—but there are some clear themes that can be consistently observed in His dealings with humanity. The primary one is that we understand the power and wonder of a personal relationship with Him.

Now, if a divine/human relationship is God's ultimate objective, how would that come about? Who does what? Given that God is the One with all the power, it would make sense that He must be the initiator. That is why His coming in human form in the person of Christ is so compelling.

But what does that mean for us today? What does Christ's coming have to say to us about the nature of God? A lot! God had essentially two options when it came to facilitating a relationship with humanity. (1) He could *force* it, or (2) He could woo us in an endeavor to *win* our affections. God wants love to be the foundation of our relationship. Therefore, He chose to win us over by the means of grace. He chose to move toward us with love (in the midst of our brokenness), so that what we bring back to Him is motivated more by gratitude than duty.

In return, God invites us to surrender to His love and to follow His way of love with one another. This is a big request. He is asking that we turn our lives over to Him and that we trust His wisdom (which often seems counterintuitive). This is a big request. That kind of request, when extended to weak, prone-to-wander human beings, necessitates a pretty significant upfront investment. A high trust request presupposes a substantial trust-inducing action on behalf of one who is truly trustworthy. God did that in a way we can never adequately repay. We will never be worthy of what He has done. And we might as well stop thinking we ever could be.

But, again, it is possible that only makes us all the more nervous about the future.

Sometimes I start thinking about all that God has done for me, and the way He has extended such amazing grace my way, and that raises the bar pretty high. God's expectations reach far beyond anything I could ever realistically live up to. So why set myself up for more disappointment?

These are very important questions. If you are wrestling with them, it is a sign that you are quite serious about this exploration process, and I hope you sense God's delight in that in and of itself.

I want to share two things that were helpful to me at this stage in my own processing.

First, it is very difficult to predict the powerful effect of grace on your own life, before you actually experience it. Looking from the outside in, you simply can't imagine what it will feel like to be truly forgiven. What it means to have a fresh start. Or how having your soul brought to life changes everything about what you know and see. It is hard to anticipate any of that. It is impossible to predict the power of it.

I can remember saying to people (just months after I had committed my life to Christ) that if someone had told me that I would walk away from the party in order to go to a Bible study, I would never have believed them. If someone had said that I would be looking forward to going to church, I would have wondered what they were smoking. If they suggested that I would be considering vocational ministry, I would have thought they were talking about someone else.

The changes that I saw in me, by the means of God's grace, surprised even me. I didn't see it coming. And it wasn't just the outward stuff. I didn't just cut my hair and stop smoking cigarettes. It wasn't just that I stopped going to parties and I started going to church. It was an internal change. My perspective changed. My desires were altered. I saw the world in a different way. I wanted different things. Some of that happened immediately, and some of it took time. And just so that I am totally open about it, some of my desires are still being changed and renewed by Him. But the change that occurred when I first embraced grace was real. I wouldn't have been able to put words to it beforehand. I couldn't have imagined it. I don't suspect that anyone can.

Second, it helped me to think about the nature of love. Let me begin from the human perspective. If a person chooses to extend love to another, and that love is rebuffed, ignored, or underappreciated, how hard is it to continue loving? It is possible, but it is certainly not fun. It is really hard to do. Maybe God is the only One who can do that. On the other hand, if you love someone, and they are genuinely appreciative of it and they attempt to reorient their lives to be responsive to it, how much more gracious are you willing to be? Even if they mess up? Even if they aren't perfect?

God willingly extended His grace when we weren't even paying attention. He was at work on our behalf when we didn't think He was even relevant. He was creating signs and signals of His reality when we were using His name in vain. If He is willing to be *that* gracious when we are busy rebuffing, ignoring, and underappreciating Him, how much more gracious will He be when we actually turn our attention toward Him?

I mess up. A lot. You will mess up. Not just by accident. On purpose. God knows this. He knows it about humanity in general. He knows it about me. He knows it about you. His grace is sufficient through it all. However, this could be a reason for great personal discouragement. But consider this: *Isn't the miracle that anything really changes at all?* Isn't it a sign of the divine at work that we make any kind of movement away from selfish ambition and vain conceit? Given the depth of our brokenness, it is a wonder that our soul even has the periodic victory. Who knows, maybe after being under His influence for a while we may even have more than just the periodic victory—and in this God's work is revealed and affirmed.

The point is, God is not waiting to send you to hell after your next mess-up. He's not! For real! But if that's true, what is hell for? Why does it even exist? Guess we have to go there, too.

Hellfire and Brimstone

As I first thought about this manuscript, I was thinking that I wouldn't address the subject of hell. Not because I don't believe it exists. Not because I was afraid that it might turn off prospective readers. The bottom line was simply that I was not really sure *how* to talk about it, and the final 10 percent is that it is still the most difficult piece of truth for me to accept.

I didn't want to reinforce stereotypical messages of an angry God excitedly sending people to hell for the smallest offense. Nor did I want to try and sound smarter or more confident on the subject than I really am. So I wish I could just sidestep it.

Yet two things compel me to write about it.

First, it occurred to me that it is important for authority figures to model some measure of being "in process" as it relates to matters of Christian doctrine. We readily say to others that it is "okay" to still be figuring stuff out along the way. But if teachers don't model some of that themselves (always appearing and sounding confident on all matters Christian), then the invitation to be in process seems a little disingenuous.

Second, I realized there are some things too important not to address—even if one does it poorly. Hell is a subject of high importance in Jesus' teaching. Jesus referred to it as a real place. It is been a matter of significant discussion throughout Church history.

My greatest difficulty with the subject of hell has to do with my own personal experiences with God. I know there is inherent danger in building one's theology around experience—because each of us (even Christians) can be so easily deceived. But the fact is that I have never ever felt anything from God that comes close to the sense of being banished to eternal damnation. I have never felt anything remotely close to that. Quite the opposite, I have only felt unending mercy and undeserved favor.

Admittedly, I have felt chastised for my foolishness. I have experienced pruning for the sake of greater fruitfulness. I have also been disciplined for my disobedience. Yet each of these experiences were tempered by a kind of grace where I knew the correction was in my best interests. So much so that when I listen to television evangelists rail on the matter of hell, or watch street preachers with their "turn or burn" placards, I simply don't have a frame of reference for what they are talking about. I even wonder sometimes if we know the same God.

The apostle Paul, who wrote most of what we have in the New Testament, had a protégé in ministry named Timothy. We have two of his mentoring letters in the New Testament. In his first letter he makes an offhanded comment that I think is extremely significant. He is encouraging Timothy to be faithful and diligent in his prayers for others, especially for leaders, and then he writes:

> *This is good and pleases God our Savior, who wants everyone to be saved and to understand the truth.* 1 Timothy 2:4, NLT

This passage ought to at least mitigate some of the rhetoric that suggests that God delights in sending people to hell. He does not. To the contrary, God is apparently making every effort to see that we avoid it.

So the place that I have landed on this doctrine, at least for now, is that God so respects our freedom to choose (giving eternal weight to our choices) that if we spend our entire life resisting grace and refusing Him, then when life is over, God simply grants us what we have always wanted—eternity without Him. God doesn't send people to hell; we send ourselves there.

The reason the Bible uses such horrific language to describe the details of this place is possibly because we are totally unaware of how much our present environment is God-sustained. Hell is a place totally devoid of God's influence, and the apocalyptic language that describes the environment is the only human way to define an eternal destination without any evidence of God's gracious presence.

As I told my son over lunch today, I may not know everything there is to know about hell, but this much I do know, it sure does sound like a place I'd like to avoid. I am also grateful that God has made provision for that avoidance—and I, for one, will gladly take full advantage of it.

But this doesn't answer the question of hell's necessity. Why hell? Frankly, I struggle with trying to hold hell and grace together. I have had such a powerful experience with grace that hell is hard to comprehend. But I would be playing loose with the scripture if I just ignored it. That might become a hard habit to break. Where would it end? If something seems uncomfortable, or inconvenient, or distasteful—should I just discount it? That seems unwise. I'm not smart enough or discerning enough to make those kinds of definitive calls.

In the end, this is something we must all ferret out—not easy, but certainly important. May God give us the capacity to walk with both integrity and humility in these matters.

The Ultimate Plunge

My youngest brother, John, accepted a temporary assignment to manage a meat-packing facility located in beautiful New Zealand. In the last year of his tenure there, he invited the whole family to join him and to spend Christmas on the beach near Mount Maunganui. We all accepted the invitation—my parents, my siblings, and their spouses, along with all of the kids. It was a year of saving pennies and finagling airline miles, but we all made the trip and it was so worth it!

One of the highlights of the vacation was an excursion we made to the Waikato River Valley and Huka Falls. Five minutes from the great lake is New Zealand's tallest bungy jump—Taupo Bungy. Not exactly sure what got into us on that particular afternoon, but my brothers, my sister, many of the kids, and several of the spouses decided to take the plunge that day.

My brother Rob was the first adult jumper. He is probably the greatest risk-taker of us all. He stood at the end of the platform looking down forty-seven meters to the blue-green water below. It is an incredible sight. But it is hard to appreciate the conflicted emotions that race around in your brain while you are standing on that platform with only a three-inch elastic band tied around your ankles. Everything inside you is saying (screaming really), *What the heck are you thinking!* It's one of those things you have to experience to appreciate.

But if you are actually going to make the jump, there comes that moment of truth, where in spite of every argument to the contrary, you must take that fateful step off the platform. My brother stood there for a few thoughtful moments, and then he did a perfect swan dive toward the water. Just before his fingers touched . . . *BOWNG* . . . he was pulled back about fifteen meters or so. He twisted and turned for a few more minutes until a lifeguard in a dinghy caught and released him from his misery just as an angler releases his fish to freedom.

After his jump, Rob made the long climb back up the wooden staircase to the platform where the next victim had already taken his place. But before my youngest brother made his leap of faith, he wanted to glean whatever insider secrets Rob might care to share on how one survives such a presumptuous and ill-advised jump. Rob, still out of breath from the long climb, was eager to share from his wealth of knowledge and experience. The breadth of his insight was summed up in a simple statement:"Oh, you'll love it! It is such a rush! But that first step is a killer!"

Yep, that first step is a killer.

My wife, Carol, stood on the platform for ten minutes and then decided she couldn't do it. She couldn't get past the stuff in her head. She had watched five of us do the dive. We gave her great advice. We cheered her on. We assured her she could do it. But nobody could make the jump for her. She had to do it for herself.

After ten minutes on the platform, she couldn't bring herself to do it. She took the harness off and went back to what she knew. She came back to solid ground.

Making the commitment to trust grace is a lot like that. Depending on your background and experience, you may find yourself standing at that platform for a long time. Leaving what is comfortable and familiar is hard to do. For some, taking a step of faith means leaving everything you have known behind—friends, reputation in the community, plans for the future—everything you have ever been or aspired to be. It leaves you wondering, *What will people think? Is this really me? What if I fail? What the heck am I thinking!*

After watching several others take their leap of faith, Carol decided to give it another try. She was sure she would regret not taking the plunge. Carol is an adventurer at heart. This experience would certainly give her a chance to lean into that side of her nature. So she went out to the platform again. Another five minutes passed. I can still picture the moment. She was in a crouched position with her arms outstretched to each side. She whispered to herself, "You can do this . . ." Then she would step back again. I tried not to feel badly for her. But, then, in a moment where inspiration surged—she jumped!

It takes some of us a little longer than others. That's okay. No shame in that. Giving the soul a chance to evolve is not for the faint of heart. The first step *is* a killer! It feels risky. But when that step is taken—the declaration made—what an adventure your soul has engaged!

DECLARE

We choose our joys and sorrows long before we experience them. —Kahlil Gibran

Think back to a time when you experienced something truly exhilarating.

- Your team won the championship. You worked really hard. You put in many hours of practice. You sacrificed while others goofed off. But when the last game was over—and you won— you felt the kind of satisfaction that comes only to those who have done what you have done. You were part of something truly amazing. Not a feeling like it!

- You graduated. Walking across the stage to receive your diploma, you found yourself reflecting on all the reasons why this shouldn't have happened. You hear the voices of the people who said that you didn't have what it took. But you did it. You persevered. You beat the odds. You have the sheepskin to prove it!

- Your wedding day. Saying the vows touched something deep inside you. In that moment you were reminded of all the times you doubted whether this day would actually come. But it happened! You felt like the luckiest person alive. It was good. It was holy. It was almost too good to be true!

- You became a parent. There is so much pain and stress throughout the birthing process. You weren't prepared for what you'd feel when it was over. Looking back now you remember being overwhelmed by the depth of your emotions as you initially locked eyes with the newborn in your arms. You felt such deep joy and daunting responsibility all at the same time!

- You received a clean bill of health. You had been worried for weeks about what the doctors would find. There were tests conducted and lab reports filed. You invited people to pray. You worried about the outcome and tried not to obsess about the worst. Then the phone call came. You were given the good news. Everything was normal. What a relief! All you could say was, "Thank God!"

There are moments that are so good and so deeply meaningful that they are etched in our memory for the rest of our lives. The ones I have just mentioned appear regularly on people's life highlight list. Let me add one that might surprise you. It is counterintuitive.

It's the day a person gets baptized.

I have had the privilege of participating in many baptismal services, and I am of the tradition that practices post-conversion full-immersion baptism. That is just a fancy way of saying that we dunk people under water after they have made a personal commitment to following Christ. Don't mean to be irreverent; I just want to be clear.

The tradition of Christian baptism goes back to the earliest days of the Church. It was a regular practice for those who made personal professions of faith to solemnize that commitment through the act of baptism. Baptism is an outward physical expression reflecting an internal spiritual reality. It is a picture of the gospel. When a person gets baptized, they are in effect joining Christ in the waters of baptism. In the same way that Jesus died, went into the grave, and rose again, so it is with a person who goes down into the water and comes out again. The old life dies. The new life is embraced. There is cleansing and renewal.

It is an incredible experience—a life highlight!

For the more skeptical this is a hard sell. For some it appears to be a meaningless religious ritual or some kind of perfunctory rite of Church initiation. Empty tradition. Religious voyeurism. Christian score-keeping.

Let me begin by acknowledging that there is always the possibility that anything good can be perverted. Not everything that is presented as holy is so. This is true in every arena of life—business, art, education, law, media, politics—you name the arena, you can find something tainted in it. The same is true when it comes to Christian practices. Christians are still human. Pastors and priests are far from perfect—even when they prefer that you believe otherwise. I don't say that to excuse the excesses. It is simply a statement of fact. Therefore, I concede that there are times and places where baptism can become (and has been) merely meaningless tradition and dead religion.

But for the sincere in faith, it is much more than that. For many who participate, it becomes a life highlight! Why? I think it has to do with the power of soul declaration. It is through baptism that the soul (and what is happening in it) takes center stage. The soul gets a chance to express itself fully—without reservation—and far from being exhibitionistic, it is a day where many attest to *things* finally being put right in their world.

So much of our lives are plagued by ambivalence. We just don't know—and that can be a very frustrating place to live. We feel tossed back and forth on the waves of double-mindedness. But when a person gets baptized, there is a moment of clarity. It is as though they are saying, "I don't know about many things, but this one thing I know. I do want to publicly declare my faith *in* and allegiance *to* Jesus Christ."

For most people the decision to be baptized is not an easy one. Typically it comes only after a significant amount of personal processing. Often people wonder if they are good enough, or knowledgeable enough, or have enough together personally to go public with their declaration of faith. But once they understand that baptism is fundamentally a declaration of intent and that it marks the beginning of a journey (and not its culmination), a person can usually allow the experience to stand on its own—to be what God designed it to be—a chance to soak (literally) in the wonder of His amazing grace.

Yet maybe this brings us to the part that is hard to understand. What is baptism *designed* to do? What is a person really *saying* when they take the plunge?

At the heart of the baptismal confession, a person affirms two truths that they are embracing as their own. First, they are acknowledging that they have personally received God's grace for the forgiveness of their sins—made available through what Christ accomplished on the cross. Second, they are declaring that they want to follow Christ as the leader of their life. He is the One they are determined to emulate. It is what Christians have historically affirmed as acknowledging Jesus as the *Lord* of their lives.

Therefore, baptism is the means by which Christ-followers affirm both a present spiritual reality and a lifelong pursuit. Rick Warren has a little saying that I think accurately reflects what is at the heart of the experience: "There is a moment of surrender and then there is the practice of surrender—which is lifelong."

Baptism captures that entire sentiment in a single act of personal submission.

What Actually Happens?

I was waist-deep in the water. My good friend, who was standing next to me, had just walked through a very painful season of his life. But as often happens in my line of work, God used the pain of his last season to introduce us to each other. Over the course of the previous few months, we had a series of spiritually significant conversations—which led to his conversion.

This was an important day. It had earned priority status in both our BlackBerries. Moments earlier I had the privilege of baptizing one of his sons, and now I was about to baptize my dear friend. The pregnant pause was full of meaning as I put my arm around his shoulder. One of our pastors read the synopsis of his story off a card he prepared beforehand. Here is what got him thinking about spiritual things in the first place . . . Here is what inspired him to cross the line of faith . . . Once the card had been read, I asked him two of the most important questions of his life.

"Have you accepted Christ as the forgiver of your sins? Is it your intent to follow Him as the Leader and Lord of your life?"

"I have . . . I do . . ."

"It is on the basis of that confession that I baptize you in the name of the Father, the Son, and the Holy Spirit."

Under the water he went.

Coming up out of the water, he heard the thunderous applause of the hundreds of people gathered at the poolside to support and celebrate his public declaration of faith. He was not the same man I met six months ago. I could see it in his eyes. I could feel it in the bear hug he gave me afterward. It was obvious in the tears shed by his family and friends who had known him much longer than I did—and witnessed firsthand the life change that the baptism simply confirmed all over again. This was a life highlight for him—and for me! We baptized thirty-seven people that day, and I believe each one of them would tell you it was an experience they will never forget.

A Declaration Toward What End?

Baptism is a life highlight. It is unforgettable. It's a spiritual mountaintop. A moment of exhilaration. However, it is just a beginning. But a beginning to what? What comes next? When Jesus was actually physically walking the face of our planet, He would invite people to be with Him through a simple invitation. He said:

"*Come, follow me . . .*" Matthew 4:19, NLT

It would make sense, wouldn't it, if a similar kind of invitation was extended to modern-day spiritual seekers. But what does that actually entail? Does it mean we don a robe, wear sandals, and become itinerant storytellers? Well, I am not sure many of us would be prompted to go that route. It's a hard way to make a living.

But, really, what is it about?

I think there is significant confusion about what it means to follow Jesus in our day. When we stop and really think about it, we probably assume it has something to do with values and lifestyle and participation in certain spiritual activities. But even there I think there is a lot of misinformation. Therefore, it might be helpful to lay it out more concretely.

I want to start by explaining what this is *not* about.

Many people, looking at this journey from the outside in, make certain assumptions about the practical implications of following Christ. These assumptions are faulty, perhaps partially because of how we view life generally.

We tend to compartmentalize life into various *slices*. Life is like a pie with various slices, with each slice representing a different role or responsibility. There is the family slice, the work slice, the health/fitness slice, the relational slice, the recreational slice, and so on.

For the person on a spiritual quest, the assumption is that we need to add another slice to the pie. Effectively, that means we must find a way to take some time and attention away from the other slices in order to make room for the soul slice. Additionally, it is assumed that really good Christians are people who have devoted the largest slice of their life to matters of the soul. For busy people with full calendars, this often seems impossible.

That is not what this is about!

The real issue—and the most fundamental spiritual battle—is about what sits at the center of our life. For most of our lives (before soul matters are important), the governing center of life is our own thoughts about what is right and good. *We* govern which slice gets the most attention. *We* determine what actually makes up the individual slices. *We* decide what defines a "good" relationship. *We* determine what we should do with our vocational aspirations. *We* make the call on the amount of time we should devote to community concerns. *We* decide what is important politically.

We don't act independently on these matters. We often take our cues from cultural norms, or what our parents taught us, or the advice of friends or books or counselors. But in the final analysis, we are always the final arbiters of what happens across the board in every area of our lives.

Becoming a follower of Jesus actually means that we willingly redraw the "lines" with a different center. We may have some of the very same slices in the pie. But we are no longer the final arbiters. We no longer take our cues from the culture or what we have determined to be right and good. Instead, we make a fundamental shift regarding the center point. We make a conscious decision to allow the values and the ways of Christ to become the governing center. Ultimately, we endeavor to heighten our sensitivity to God's work within us, so that increasingly our whole life takes on the flavor of Christ-likeness.

Paul wrote about this in his letter to the Romans, when he penned these words:

So here's what I want you to do, God helping you: Take your everyday, ordinary life—your sleeping, eating, going-to-work, and walking-around life—and place it before God as an offering. Embracing what God does for you is the best thing you can do for him. Don't become so well-adjusted to your culture that you fit into it without even thinking.

Instead, fix your attention on God. You'll be changed from the inside out. Romans 12:1–2, MSG

Perhaps this explanation brings some relief, because there is at least some rhyme and reason to what is expected. It isn't just a magical mystery tour—Jesus style. Yet at the same time, it could feel a little disconcerting, because at the end of the day we all really kinda like calling the shots. We like being in control. We are not usually very good at allowing the evolving soul (governed by Christ's admonitions) to have increased influence on what, how, and why we do what we do. It's hard for me. I suspect it would be hard for you, too.

The difficulty of that proposition causes me to come back to three basic truths that I review almost every day of my life. I still have to consciously remind myself of these things, even though I have been on this path for many years.

1. God knows more than I do. He also has my best interests at heart, even when the circumstances of my life don't confirm that reality (in the ways I would prefer). He is *always* at work for good. I can trust His wisdom, His intentions, and His aspirations for me and my future—it is what I truly want.

2. I consistently make a mess of things when I am in control. I am not always intentionally rebellious. Sometimes I try to be right and do good, but I simply don't have the right information or the right perspective or enough power to make the best choices for myself and the people I care about.

3. I can choose whether or not to trust God's ways. He will not force me to do His bidding. I can always choose to do my own thing. I can still exert my own will—and face those consequences. He is the perfect gentleman and waits for me to willingly relinquish my ways for His.

A Daily Declaration

Essentially, I wake up every day making a very similar declaration to the one I made at my baptism. I accept Christ's forgiveness for my missteps and lack of trust (because I am still very much in process), *and* I reaffirm my intent to follow Him as the Leader and Lord of my life.

Specifically, it means that I am paying attention to those areas of my life that are out of sync with what I am learning about the ways and manners of Jesus. Quite frankly, that is usually not all that hard to figure out. This is one of those places where natural insight and spiritual insight partner together serendipitously.

When I talk about the natural, I am suggesting that there are some areas of my life that are obviously in need of work. I know the challenge before me, because it is the place where my life is most out of control. It is the area that I *know* needs work. It is what keeps me up at night and what my friends and family worry about the most.

My friends at Natural Church Development introduced me to a great organizational word picture that I think has an application on a personal level, as well. Consider a barrel made of wooden staves. Imagine each stave is a different length. As you fill the barrel with water, it leaks at the point of the shortest stave. Our lives are a lot like that. There is much that God wants to pour into us, and the limiting factor is the area of weakness or challenge represented by the shortest stave. It could be a matter of addiction. It could be a relational challenge. It could be a matter of personal ethics. It could be a secret sin. It could be a debilitating attitude. Or it could be an unresolved pain from the past.

The place of greatest challenge is the place where God's Spirit usually wants to begin His work. You don't have to make it any more complicated than that. Sometimes people want to spiritualize things by assuming there is something much deeper that needs to be addressed—and don't worry, that is coming. But deal with that which is most obvious first, and trust that God will reveal the other layers in due time.

But the hard part is that solutions don't come easy. Observing and determining the most pressing issue/challenge/need may be quite natural (obvious), but figuring out what to do about it is not. Yet this brings us to the heart of spiritual transformation.

This is key!

Fundamentally, all of life's challenges and opportunities are soul matters—even if it doesn't seem like it. This is what I meant when I suggested that following Jesus involved having a different governing center. It is a personal recognition that if I am going to make headway in any area of my life, I understand its connection to what is happening inside. I embrace the fact that every issue is a spiritual issue.

Therefore, when it comes to dealing with my personal challenges and weaknesses, I address them all from a spiritual perspective. This doesn't mean that there aren't pragmatic steps to take—there are. But I start with a spiritual center. I work through every arena of life by paying attention to what is happening in my soul. I listen. I reflect. I try and figure out how to channel the longings, desires, and decisions in a God-ward direction. Ronald Rolheiser captures this so well when he writes:

> "Long before we do anything explicitly religious at all, we have to do something about the fire that burns within us. What we do with that fire, how we channel it, is our spirituality. Thus, we all have a spirituality whether we want one or not."

Let me pause right there. I want to give you a moment to think about that, because the rest of this book teases out what that looks like from a Christian perspective.

Reinforcing the Declaration

Okay, time for another personal confession.

One of my pet peeves (especially regarding matters of the soul) is when people make this process sound easier than it is. When someone says "just do this and that" and you'll be fine, I am tempted to cuss. I know, I know, not very Christian of me. But it really bugs me, because it is simply not true. The process of moving toward spiritual maturity is really hard. It is messy. Invariably you will take two steps forward and one step back—and sometimes even one step forward and two steps back. That is true for everyone, and I wish we would all be more forthcoming about that.

The reason I bring that up now is because what I am about to do may seem like a direct contradiction. I am going to try to summarize a lifelong spiritual transformation process in a few paragraphs. However, because I am trying to be efficient with my words does not mean that I think the process is easy or non-demanding. It is heart-wrenching. But necessary! So what I want to do here is provide a basic road map, the details of which I will fill in from this point forward.

As I think about my own path of following Jesus, it has revolved around a threefold process that happens on multiple levels in my life. It isn't necessarily linear, in that I moved from step one to step two, etc. It is much more circular and interactive. But each of these three components were/are always involved.

Information—Making progress in my spiritual journey has always required a diligent pursuit of good information. Our souls will not evolve without it. Therefore, in the same way that I attend to feeding my body, I am responsible to find nourishment for my soul.

I find the eating analogy helpful, because in the same way that we would say that quality food matters when it comes to our bodies, quality "food" matters when it comes to the nourishment of our soul as well. We have to be discerning about that which we feed the soul. Not everything bearing the title "spiritual" is automatically soul-worthy. We do well to evaluate the source.

In this regard, let me make a comment about the importance of the Bible. Without going into a long explanation about why I have found this to be such a relevant and helpful tool, let me just suggest that you engage it for yourself before you make any final judgments about its value. Most of the people whom I have talked to, who are Bible critics, simply haven't spent that much time with it. Conversely, many of those who read it and make a regular practice of studying it come away from the experience helped and spiritually nourished.

This doesn't mean that there aren't portions of the scripture that are difficult. This doesn't mean that you are not allowed to have questions about those places where science and scripture collide. We all wrestle with that. The salient point for me is that the Christ-followers I most respect unapologetically endorse the value of the Bible in their own growth and spiritual evolution. In addition, in my most honest moments I *know* I need an authoritative reference point to evaluate the quality of the information I am processing. I have consistently found the Bible invaluable in that regard.

Reflection—It is not the gathering of information alone that nurtures spiritual growth. Gleaning good information is often the necessary starting point. However, it is when quality information is assimilated and reflected on that it has the intended effect. Consider this: We live in an information-rich society. We have access to so much. As a result, we can become information junkies. We can always be learning but never really acknowledging the truth.

This has led to an interesting (and disturbing) phenomenon in modern-day Christianity. We know more than we can usually apply. We equate head knowledge about spiritual matters with spiritual maturity. The tragedy in all this is that we get set up for spiritual pride, which is perhaps the greatest impediment to spiritual maturation. The Scriptures regularly remind us that God actually opposes the proud, but He extends grace to the humble. The practice of reflection fosters the development of humility.

But let me be candid enough to say that there isn't much in our culture that will aid us in this discipline. The pace at which we do life works against us. In fact, it may be that this is one of the least talked about and most indispensable dynamics in the spiritual evolutionary process.

The major difference between self-help and soul evolution has to do with the working of God's Spirit. It takes time to quiet the noise of our lives long enough to heed the whispering of the voice of God. I find it hard enough to distinguish God's voice from all the other voices of my life—even knowing the importance of reflection. So if I didn't take the time to do it, it would be hopeless. Unfortunately, many well-meaning followers of Jesus are so consumed with knowing more that they miss the ways in which God might want to speak to them about what is actually most important (in that moment).

Application—This is the final piece of the process. This involves engaging the will. It moves our spiritual pursuit from theory to practice. In many ways this is where the battle is ultimately won or lost. The primary challenge here—especially early on—is that we are weak. We have developed certain ways of thinking and living that are not soul-friendly. Some of us have been doing what we have been doing for a long time. Change is hard even when we know what to do. So this is where I take a lot of comfort and solace in the admonition that Jesus gave to His original disciples.

> *"Watch and pray so that you will not fall into temptation. The spirit is willing, but the body is weak."* Matthew 26:41, NIV

The truth is, God knows our makeup, and He understands that we are weak-willed. He knows the ambivalence inherent in the human nature, and how hard it is for us to change. He is full of mercy and compassion. More importantly, He has provided His Spirit to enable us to do what we cannot do on our own. One of the most hopeful promises in all of scripture is found in Romans 8:

> *If the Spirit of him who raised Jesus from the dead is living in you, he who raised Christ from the dead will also give life to your mortal bodies through his Spirit, who lives in you.* Romans 8:11, NIV

This doesn't mean I will never fail. I can still refuse to cooperate. But (and this is a very important "but"), I have access to a powerful ally that gives me reason for hope. I don't have to do what I have always done. I don't have to be what I have always been. God is at work in me both to will and do His bidding. This is the promise my soul holds to as the reason and means for ultimate triumph. I never want to let it go. It has become my life. Perhaps it is to be the hope of your life as well.

HOLD

"Ahhh, yes, apparently you know how to take the reservation. You just don't know how to hold the reservation—and that's really the most important part of the reservation: the holding. Anybody can just take 'em!" —Jerry Seinfeld

The meaning of some words can change over time. Ironically some words can even change dramatically. A word that had positive connotations in one time period can carry negative connotations in another.

The word *disciple* is like that.

Disciple is not really a term we use a lot in our modern everyday language. If we do use it, it is usually in a derogatory way. On CNN we might hear someone referred to as a disciple of David Koresh. The image that is portrayed is that a disciple is an individual who is more or less brainwashed, socially inept, and totally out of touch with reality—in short, a modern-day reject. This is hardly something we would aspire to become.

So as soon as someone begins to come to some understanding about God, and they say "Okay, let's go. I'm ready to get serious about my faith!" a well-meaning Christian leader might say, "Great, now it is time to get on with your discipleship process." The new Christ-follower often finds themselves thinking, *Whoa, wait a minute, not sure I am ready to go there!* And it's all because of the baggage surrounding the word—and not necessarily the process itself.

I'd like to try to set the record straight.

The word *disciple* was commonly used in Jesus' day. To be a disciple simply meant to be an "avid student." The Pharisees had their *disciples*. John the Baptist had his *disciples*. And, of course, Jesus had His *disciples* as well. It was actually a position of privilege. To be chosen as a disciple of a noted leader or teacher was an honor. In some cases there was a rigorous application process. Think Rush Week in college. Multiply that by a factor of ten and you'll start to get the picture of what this was really like in those days—in a more moral and righteous sort of way (of course).

Perhaps the closest modern parallel is the process of apprenticeship—and I'm not talking about a reality show that Donald Trump might concoct. Rather, if you want to learn a trade or a craft, one of the ways to master the skill is to learn everything you can from an expert in the field. You learn by watching and experimenting. You are tutored and mentored. Then, after many years of study, you yourself become a master craftsman.

There is nothing bizarre or funky about this arrangement. You don't turn off your brain. You don't have to drink the magic Kool-Aid. Quite the opposite! You engage the brain, you ask questions, and you develop your own style. Perhaps most importantly you are determined to be disciplined about the process—hence the word *disciple*.

Becoming a disciple of Jesus is very much about that. You come to recognize the excellency of the Master's work. As a result, you find yourself saying, "I want to train myself to become more like Him. I want to learn from Him. I want to do life the way He proscribes." The greatest compliment for you would be when someone says, "I can see something of the Master's influence on your life." That is what is meant by discipleship. It is a spiritual transformation process that occurs through training ourselves in His ways. Through learning, reflection, experimentation, and regular disciplined submission to the leadings and promptings of God's Spirit, we become more like Him in that unique way we were designed to reflect Him.

Why This Is Hard

I have a practice (on most mornings) to set aside some time to make a personal connection with God. I understand that being a modern-day disciple of Jesus involves my whole day, but I like to (and need to) spend some focused time with God as I get ready for my day.

The routine I use is pretty straightforward. I spend some time reading the Bible, usually something out of the Psalms, Proverbs, or the teachings of Jesus. It is not typically an in-depth study; it's just a way to focus my thoughts. I have a favorite chair by the fireplace. I keep a journal on the table next to the chair. When I finish my reading, I write a few reflections on what I have read, and how it might connect to my life. Then I sit in silence, and ask if there is anything else the Lord might want to speak to my soul. I try to sit still for ten minutes.

As I describe this routine, it sounds so easy—doesn't it? Everybody can do at least that much. Right? Not so much. It is actually a battle. I used to think that it was just me. I would hear pastors and other Christian leaders talk about deeply meaningful devotional experiences and how they love to spend time in the Word. I would read biographies of great Christians from days of old, who would get up at 4 A.M. to pray for an hour. I have trouble staying focused for twenty minutes. Truth is, there are many days when I don't even feel like doing it all—and I don't. And I'm a pastor!

What's wrong with me?

The spiritual journey is hard, because it's hard. Maintaining a meaningful relationship with God is work because it is a work of faith. It is unlike anything else we do. We can't count on our senses in the same way that we can in every other area of our lives. There are also many things working against us. We get bored. We feel odd. The Scriptures teach that there are even forces of darkness that exact their price. In fact, despite the oft-repeated cliché, it *doesn't* get easier with time.

Here is why it's consistently hard for me.

Frustration over mixed messages. One of the things that happens in Christian circles is that people use vocabulary and catch phrases where it is assumed that everyone knows what is being discussed. One of those phrases is, "God spoke to me . . ." We use that phrase to describe an impression that we have had that we believe has divine origins. But sometimes we use it because we want to insulate an idea from discussion. It is hard to argue with something that *God* has said. Sometimes we just want to sound more spiritual than we really are. Sometimes God has really spoken. But how do discern between all these possibilities?

The fact is, I am not always sure if what I am "hearing" is truly from God. I will have moments in my morning devotions (during my silence) when I have an impression—a thought that seems "bigger" than something I could come up with on my own. In the moment, I think it could be a prompting from the Lord. I am not sure. I think it is—especially if it seems consistent with what I just finished reading from the Bible.

On my good days, I will act on that impression (in faith that it was indeed placed in my soul by God). If the action has a positive net result (in the way that I typically measure good results), then I will feel more confident talking about the impression as something from the Lord. I will find myself saying things like, "God spoke to me about calling a friend to see if they needed prayer. It was so cool, because they said they were just asking God for some confirmation on a decision they were making—and my call was a sign that God heard his prayer!" Then, whomever I am talking to might give me a high-five, and one of us would say, "Isn't God cool like that!"

Early on in my journey with God, that kind of thing seemed to happen a lot. God seemed to be talking to me all the time.

But here's the dilemma. After years of walking the path, I also have an ever-increasing list of experiences where the impressions I received (and acted upon) didn't seem to work out as well.

- I felt impressed to join a small group Bible study. It was a dud.

- I felt impressed to invite a friend to church. He came and he hated it.

- I felt impressed to pray for a sick sibling. They ended up in the hospital.

- I felt impressed to volunteer for an event. No one called me back.

And it is not just the minor disappointments; there are the biggies, too.

- I felt impressed to make a large donation to the church's building campaign, and the stock market crashed.

- I felt impressed to make a sacrificial commitment to serve a social service organization. But my ideas are rebuffed and my motivations are questioned.

- I felt impressed to make an investment in a troubled teen. After six months he is back on drugs and the parents blame me for not doing enough.

What is someone supposed to do with experiences like that? How do you respond to the next impression you think might be from the Lord? Has God really spoken? Is it just me? Am I just looking at the wrong results? Just because I obey a prompting, does that mean that everything is guaranteed to work out like I hope it will? Am I the only one who has these kinds of experiences? I can't imagine that's true, so why isn't anyone else talking about it? Why do we only hear the testimonials where God comes through in obvious and miraculous ways? It almost makes it sound like that's the norm, but if it doesn't happen, what went wrong? Did you not have enough faith? Is that true? I don't always have enough faith . . .

It just seems to get *more* complicated—and yes, frustrating—the longer I am around this stuff. Not less so. Perhaps that is part of what makes the devotional chair harder to find on some mornings.

It is a fearful and complicated matter to engage the God of the universe.

Loss of spiritual feelings. From early on in my journey, communion was always a very meaningful experience for me. Communion is a time (usually in the context of a worship service) when Christ-followers reflect on the sacrifice of Christ using the symbolism of bread and wine. I was mentored by pastors and Christian leaders who infused the celebration with such rich meaning. I could not wait to participate. Taking the bread and drinking from the cup was a reminder of the commitments I had made at my baptism. I felt God's presence in ways I could not deny.

I have also been fortunate enough to bask in the goodness of meaningful singing experiences under worship leaders who were tremendously gifted. It wasn't just their musical skill. There was more to it. They seemed to have a direct link to heaven, and when they started singing they brought the entire room with them into the presence of the Lord. It was palpable.

There have been seasons when I have been in the midst of making some very difficult decisions that affected the lives of many people. I understand what it means to "labor in prayer" on a matter. I can also remember when in the midst of those heart-wrenching circumstances I sensed a peace in my soul that was unexplainable. The weight of the decision merited anxiety, fear, and desperation. But I felt rest and peace. I knew it was God.

It is wonderful to have emotional affirmations that confirm the reality of what you believe. But again, the longer you are at the journey, the more you experience the other side as well. Your mind wanders as you take communion. You are easily distracted by the outfit the backup singer is wearing. You fast and pray and you get nothing.

We all understand that is in the nature of relationships for feelings to come and go. It's true in marriage. It's true in friendship. It's true with business partners. It's true between roommates. We all understand that. There are good days and bad days. It is what it is.

But with God it seems different. We can't see Him. We can't touch Him. We can't hear Him speak audibly—at least I haven't. So when we can't *feel* Him—what do we have to go on? How do we know it's real? Has He left us? Have we left Him? Have we done something so wrong that He no longer wants anything to do with us?

Finding my familiar spot by the fireplace (with my Bible, journal, and ten minutes of silence) means I have to sit with all of that. I Don't always want to go there! Besides, there is a bunch of paperwork on my desk at the office that really needs my attention. I really should go in early today . . . tomorrow . . . the rest of the week.

Nagging questions and doubts. I think many people assume that spiritual seekers have most of their doubts at the beginning of their journey. I'm not so sure. When a person begins their search for God, it is often prompted by an awareness that what they are presently doing is not working. Usually there is some fairly severe personal pain associated with the launch of the search. A person is facing the backlash of poor decisions, or the heartache of a broken relationship, or the realization that life has spun out of control. They are looking for relief.

The promise of grace, forgiveness, and a new beginning can be very appealing to a person in this position. That is not to say that they don't have to work through certain issues foundational to putting their faith in Christ. But I think it is fair to say that the reality of the "pain factor" and the hope for something different keeps things moving in a positive spiritual direction. God, in His mercy, meets many of us at exactly that point.

However, let's fast-forward a year or two (or twenty). God has been gracious. A new start is granted. Forgiveness and renewal have come. The pain has subsided. Life achieves some semblance of normalcy. With the immediate crisis over, the questions and doubts that were pushed to the background can now start making their way to the surface. Add some frustration over mixed messages and the loss of spiritual feelings, and you have the makings of a perfect spiritual storm.

It can take people out. It can take people out that we least expect.

I will never forget the day I had my first encounter with such a story. It marked me as a thirteen-year-old kid. We had just been to church and my parents called the five children into the living room. We sat down wondering what all the fuss was about. My dad had an important announcement. He cleared his throat. He said, "I have made an important decision." He paused. "I won't be going to church with you anymore."

What?

This was earth-shaking news. My dad was very active in church throughout my growing-up years. He was serious about it. Remember baseball on Sunday? He was also on the board of deacons, he sang in the choir, and my parents hosted a small group in our home every other Friday night. So this was a monumental shift for him.

When we asked him why, he said, "Well, with your mom's illness I have spent a lot of time praying and asking God to heal her, and she just hasn't gotten any better." My mom had been in and out of the hospital for a number of years struggling with depression. He continued, "I have begun to question my faith. I am not even sure God exists anymore. At the very least, I just don't think He is who I always thought Him to be. I am not going to go to church pretending to believe something I just can't buy anymore. I'm not going to be a hypocrite." Outside of weddings and funerals and an occasional special event, that was the last time he went to church.

As I sat there listening to his unexpected turnabout, I was dumbfounded. My dad was giving up on church and God? Whoa! But then I thought to myself, *Maybe I won't have to go anymore either!* That day became a turning point of sorts for me as well.

One of the main reasons I wanted to write this book is because I don't think there is enough conversation happening regarding the complexity of spiritual maturity—and the challenges that come with living out the Christian faith authentically. I don't mean that as a slight against anyone in particular. Maybe there is more conversation happening than I realize, but perhaps there should be more. Perhaps we would be helped by the candor. I feel compelled to alert us all to the reality of the struggle that goes with doing this for a lifetime. It's an engaging message. It's a thrilling journey. But it is not an easy life. Jesus never said it would be.

But maybe you already knew that. Maybe I am just telling your story—different words but a similar plot.

What Are the Options?

I have been helping spiritual seekers for most of my adult life. I have found it extremely rewarding (and challenging) to walk an honest path with people who are attempting to understand and live their lives with spiritual integrity. When it gets hard I have watched people choose one of three options.

Option One—*Punt*

My dad came to this conclusion. His life and his beliefs could not remain congruent. Something had to give. It was his faith. I respect my dad immensely. He was a good man. He was a faithful husband and father. I admire the fact that he didn't just play the part of devoted churchman. He was real.

I suspect there are seasons of life when we all feel like punting. *Hard* is not just a word. When you are experiencing "hard" we call it that because we feel confused and frustrated. Things aren't making sense. We are not sure we can make it. What is being asked of us seems beyond us. Everything within us is wanting to bail. It isn't worth it. This is too hard. Punt!

The thing that keeps me on my path is that I really haven't discovered a better option. I am reminded of the story out of the life of Jesus. He had been speaking to the crowds, and what He said was very difficult for them to hear. He gave one of His hard teachings. Many people stopped following that day. Lots of folks punted. Jesus turned to His disciples and asked them if they were going to leave as well. I so resonate with how Peter answered.

> *"Lord, to whom would we go? You have the words that give eternal life."* John 6:68, NLT

If I punt, I am back where I started. I am left again to my own devices. I am back to my own understanding and perspective on life. I know where that leads. I have been there and done that. I don't want that. I can't go back to that. Punting is not an option for me.

Option Two—*Pretend*

The much more common response, to the harder parts of the journey, is the decision to play a religious game with God. The hardship lowers our trust. Therefore, people draw certain conclusions about God during their season of hardship and they decide that God can't be trusted in certain areas.

Perhaps they have been hurt relationally, so from that point on relationships become the area where they will retain control. They think to themselves, *I don't want to experience that kind of hardship again. God can't be trusted with this area of my life. So I am going to do my own thing in this arena.* They may still go to church. They may still put money in the offering plate. They may still pray and use religious language. But their hearts have been compartmentalized again in a way where they have begun to move themselves back to the center of the pie, at least in certain areas.

All of this happens very subtly. It is not something that people typically talk about. It is very much an internal deal. Depending on the hardship people have experienced, the shift can take on different characteristics. For some it is about trusting God with their finances. They have been burned, so they can't release their need for control. For some it is about trusting God with the future. They tried something that didn't work, so now they have to determine what's next. Name the slice of life where you have experienced your greatest disappointment, and this will be the place where it will be most tempting to take back ownership.

On an emotional level, I totally get it. I understand why we want to reassert our influence. It makes total sense in the moment. We are convinced that this is the only way things will ever work out right. But we have to stop and think about what we are saying when we do that. Essentially, we are asserting that we know more than God. We are smarter than God in certain arenas of life. To say it out loud reveals just how ludicrous it really is. We don't know more than God. His ways are always higher and better than ours. It makes no sense to play games with Him.

In fact, doesn't it stand to reason that if we try to take back control (in whatever area), hoping that it will protect us from future hardship—doesn't that actually open us for deeper and more profound pain? Control is an illusion. We all have limited understanding and capacity. If we continue doing what we have always done (trying to manage our own success), we will continue getting what we have always gotten. Is that what we really want? Does that really effectively insulate us from future hardship? Can playing games with God ever really lead to a good outcome?

Option Three—*Persevere*

Perseverance is about deliberately putting one foot in front of the other. It is about trusting when trusting is hard. It is about holding on to the goodness of God's character and intentions, even when the circumstances of our life are screaming that we ought to do otherwise.

How do people do that?

I am not exactly sure how others do it. But for me, I always find myself coming back to a fundamental question about the nature of the journey itself. I find myself coming back to the confession I made at my baptism and how I reaffirmed it every time I have took communion. Whose journey is this—really?

Who is leading?

Is this fundamentally *my* journey, where I try to get God to endorse my plans, my ideas, and fulfill my agenda? On the most basic level, is life about getting God to bless my dreams or is it about me blessing His?

When I got baptized, it was relatively easy to say that I wanted to do things *His* way. I wanted to bless *His* plan. All I had to offer God was my messy life that wasn't working very well. But as the years have passed, there is more at stake. I have a family, and a job, and expectations about what "goodness" means for me. I have experiences with God that have made things more complicated and less comfortable. So the question of leadership—giving God permission to lead my life—is much more complex the longer I am on the path. I don't know that we can answer this question once and for all. I think we have to answer this question regularly. Perhaps even daily.

One of the first verses from the Bible that I was introduced to is a passage out of the Old Testament. It quickly became my favorite.

"For I know the plans I have for you," declares the LORD, "plans to prosper you and not to harm you, plans to give you hope and a future." Jeremiah 29:11, NIV

I was drawn to this text because of the promise. The idea that God had plans for my prosperity and future grabbed me. The fact that His plans were not about taking life from me, but giving hope to me, seemed too good to be true. I was hooked! However, the longer I have been on this journey, the more I have noticed the first portion of the passage.

The word of the Lord to the prophet emphasizes the idea that God is the One with the plan. "I know the plans *I* have for you . . ." God is leading. In fact, the broader context suggests that the whole reason God encourages Jeremiah with these words is because the circumstances in Jeremiah's life are not consistent with the promise. Jeremiah's situation was such that it would be easy to conclude that God *is* about destruction and the removal of hope.

So God extends the hope-filled promise in the midst of these difficult circumstances. It is almost as though God is saying, "I know it may look like this is not true. But let Me remind you of something. I have a plan for you. It is not to destroy you, though it may feel like it right now. The plan is good. Prosperity and hope are central to it, though not in the way you probably expect it. So trust Me. Don't punt. Don't pretend. Persevere!"

That is what I want to do! Don't you? I want to persevere.

But even when I know what I want to do, I have trouble pulling it off by myself. I think everyone does. Maybe that is why we need—and it's okay to admit it—a little help from our friends.

TRANSITIONS

CHURCH

O God,
make of me some nourishment
for these starved times,
some food
for my brothers and sisters
who are hungry for gladness and hope,
that, being bread for them,
I may also be fed
and be full. —Ted Loder

It's time for another personal confession. I often feel very much alone in this battle. Often I think I am the only one who is having trouble, spiritually speaking. Other people must figure this stuff out much more easily. Other people don't struggle as much as I do. Maybe that is true.

However, there are also moments, and usually it is later at night after a glass or two of wine, when I am sitting on the couch with a fellow Christ-follower, and we start talking about the real stuff of life. Sometimes one of us will crack the door open with a question like, "How is it really going?"

Usually there is a long pause.

Thoughts bounce back and forth. *Should I be honest? People don't like complainers! Everyone has it rough in one way or another. Don't burden them. But they seem genuinely interested . . .*

Occasionally I press past all the mental gymnastics and I take a risk. I let someone see what is really happening in my soul. More often than not, I discover I am not alone. I discover that other people have the same questions I do. Sometimes they will say something profound and helpful. Sometimes just knowing that someone else is struggling provides perspective. It is truly amazing what can happen in the course of an hour-long conversation.

You see you are not as alone as you thought.

You experience people who care.

You feel loved.

Hmmm, maybe I need a spiritual community after all.

It's a nice thought, but here is my problem. I am not an institutional guy. I am a rebel at heart. Rules and I have never really gotten along so well. I have never found a rule that I wasn't tempted to break. I ride a Harley. I wear an earring. I have a large, conspicuous tattoo on my arm.

Yet I am a pastor. I love working with people. I have a master's degree in biblical studies. I also have an MBA.

I went to business school because I believed that a good understanding of management would help increase my overall effectiveness. I enjoyed learning how to coalesce and leverage resources in order to achieve a mission. I was fascinated by how functional structures could facilitate efficiency—to release and focus people to make their best contribution. I became intrigued by the magic of servant-oriented leadership, and determined to adopt that manner as my own.

But institutions make me nervous. Institutions are bureaucratic. Institutions stifle creativity. They take on a life of their own. They have a tendency to kill the spirit of the people who founded them. I find it ironic that I ended up in the Church. It is the institution to end all institutions, is it not? But perhaps God, with His own sense of irony, loves facilitating interesting contradictions. Maybe He actually enjoys inviting people like me to church.

But what is the Church?

In the English language we use the word *church* to mean at least five different things. Surprisingly, I don't think most people are aware of what they are talking about as they use the word. Not out of ignorance or irreverence per se. Rather, I think for many people, it all runs together into one big ol' religious blob. The mental images are all connected—sort of—but the lack of clarity about what we are really discussing has some pretty serious ramifications.

Is it the building?

Sometimes we use the word *church* to refer to a physical structure. If people travel abroad and they get to tour a beautiful cathedral, how do they talk about the experience when they come home?

"We saw such beautiful churches in Europe!"

"Or is it the worship service? "

Other times we use the word *church* to describe the worship experience itself. When a family gets back in the car after a Sunday morning event, they start driving home, and someone invariably asks the question: "So, what did you think of church today?"

Or is it the organizational entity that dispenses spiritual services?

If you have a friend who is going through a difficult time— maybe they are experiencing marital trouble, or a financial crisis, or they're dealing with an addiction—and you want to be of help (but you don't know who to call), you might suggest: "Hey, let's call the church!"

Or is it the collection of doctrines that define prescribed beliefs of the adherents?

If you are engaged in a discussion about a particular social, moral, or political issue, it is not unusual for someone to make a statement reflecting what they believe to be a general sentiment held by Christians. They might say: "The church is so out-of-touch on that matter!"

Or is it a specific congregation?

When someone wants to identify personally with a group of Christians who have organized themselves around a particular mission and vision, and this person wants to formalize their affiliation, he/she might ask: "How do I join this church?"

On the surface it seems like such a simple thing to talk about—the Church. But what are we actually talking about? Are we talking about a building? A Sunday morning event? A service-providing entity? A set of beliefs? A local congregation?

If there wasn't enough confusion surrounding the word itself, we also have history to deal with—both personal and global. People have varying emotional reactions to the concept of *church*, depending on their personal experiences and their general perceptions of its value over time.

Is the Church a good thing? It depends on what we are talking about. It depends on your own personal experience with it. It depends on how you evaluate its influence in history. Does the good outweigh the bad? Put that all together and there are probably as many opinions about the Church (with varying levels of intensity) as people you ask about it.

So let's go back to its beginning.

When we go back to the earliest biblical manuscripts, the word *church* is used almost exclusively as a reference to the community of faith. The word translated "church" comes from the Greek word *ekklesia*, which literally means "called out (together) ones." This is one of those places where etymology has real value.

First, there is the sense that the Church is "called out" for a purpose. There is a mission that God has in mind. We are called to be with Him, to honor Him, to be changed by Him, and to reflect Him to the world at large.

Second, there is the expectation and calling to "togetherness," or community. There is a standard set for relational intimacy that goes beyond mere affinity. The love dynamic of the community is commissioned to be of such quality that the world would be in awe of what it saw.

Third, and perhaps this is the most obvious, it is about people. The Church is all about the people who gather and serve in Christ's name. It is *not* about the buildings, or services, or even the various moral or political positions held by those who participate.

In short, the Church is God's people doing God's thing!

The reason I have gone to such great lengths to explain this, is because from here on out I am going to be talking about our spiritual journey in relation to a faith community. The first part of the book has been focused on what happens inside us as we endeavor to be faithful to our soul's evolution. However, this second part is focused on what happens in the context of community—the Church.

I didn't want you to be confused about what I was thinking as I write about the Church. I want to be clear about what I am inviting you to engage in.

Another problem (perhaps the bigger problem) is that I don't know how any of this strikes you personally. You may be very open and receptive to the prospect of Church life. You have no strong reactions against it. You may be thinking, *I don't understand what all the fuss is about. Let's just go!*

Or you could be on the opposite end of the spectrum. In fact, if the research conducted by David Kinnaman and Gabe Lyons (synthesized in a book entitled *unchristian*) is reflective of your thoughts, you are probably disturbed by what you see. You are part of the growing population that sees the Church as the last thing in the world you want to consider. Perhaps you share the negative sentiments of the disgruntled *outsiders* they interviewed. One man they spoke to was rather blunt:

Christianity has become bloated with blind followers who would rather repeat slogans than actually feel true compassion and care. Christianity has become marketed and streamlined into a juggernaut of fear-mongering that has lost its own heart.

Therefore, it may be inconceivable for you to imagine being associated with a group of Christ-followers that you would enjoy. You have been jaded by the hypocrisy of Christians, burned by the scandalous sins of certain leaders, and put off by the pettiness of people who insist on making mountains out of molehills. Not to mention the politics!

Church—no thank you!

Nevertheless I have a big request to make. Regardless of your perceptions and experience, I want to invite you to find a place of openness. The evolution of your soul may just depend on it!

The Church *is* an imperfect place, because it *is* comprised of imperfect people. The good news is that it can also be used supernaturally by God to bring about healing, encouragement, strength, perspective, joy, and a positive change in the world at large. As with any human endeavor, the Church is only as strong and vibrant as the people who are in it. So, it is okay if you are wary. It is okay if you are cautiously optimistic. The reality is that your engagement in community will be messy and soul-satisfying all at the same time. It is good. It is what we all need. It is where God is inviting us.

God bless your soul as you embark on your adventure in the Church. Perhaps you will be fortunate to discover—as I did—that there is a wonderful surprise awaiting you.

OUR STORY

TRUST

He who does not trust enough, will not be trusted. —Lao Tzu

My sister wrote a poem when she was twelve years old. It was birthed out of watching my mom work through the emotional anguish of having suffered the ravages of war as a prisoner in a Japanese internment camp.

Never Ending Hell
> *A young child,*
> *Sitting among soldiers, weapons and hatred.*
> *An innocent bystander to violent deaths.*
> *A young mind growing old too soon.*
>
> *A young woman,*
> *Sitting with her friends,*
> *Not talking out the hurt*
> *Not talking out the horror.*
>
> *A middle-aged mother,*
> *Sitting in a psychological institution,*

Finally talking out the hurt,
Finally talking out the horror.

An elderly woman
Sitting among her kin
Mad at the war for her life full of hurting,
Angry at the war for her life full of horror.

A young daughter,
Not comprehending her mother's hurt
Not understanding her mother's horror.

A teenage daughter,
Confused by her mother's hurt,
Baffled by her mother's horror.

A middle-aged mother,
Sad for her mother whom the war hurt,
Upset for her mother whom the war caused horror.

A young child,
Sitting among soldiers, weapons and hatred . . .

My grandfather (my mother's father) taught in a Christian college in Indonesia. It was a teacher's college. When Japan invaded Indonesia, many of the Dutch immigrants were placed in camps. My mom spent four horrible years in such a camp. When the war was over, everybody was thrilled to have survived. Thrilled to be free. No one wanted to rehash the pain of the past. "Don't even think about it" was the message they all obeyed. "Just relish the fact that you made it through." That worked for twenty years.

My parents met in Indonesia after the war. After moving back to the Netherlands, they were married in 1956, they had their first child in 1957, and immigrated to the United States in 1959. They settled on the East Coast, living the normal American life—going to church, planning picnics, loving baseball, and at the risk of sounding totally cliché, my mom also made a killer apple pie. A normal happy family.

All of that changed after my mom lost her sixth child. My youngest brother, Paul, died two weeks after he was born because of medical complications. Afterward my mom slipped into a debilitating depression that lasted for almost ten years. At first we assumed that the depression was a result of the lost child. It is a terrible thing to lose a baby. Who wouldn't be depressed?

But with the help of good doctors and lots of talking, she discovered that her depression was actually rooted in painful unresolved memories that had long been buried. After the war, she determined never to talk about what happened. She bought into the misguided notion that the most efficient way to deal with pain is to stuff it. It worked for a while. You have probably noticed that, too—stuffing can work for a while. But the loss of Paul became the emotional tipping point where stuffing no longer worked.

Stuffing pain is an impossible way to do life long term. It inhibits love—both its giving and receiving—because all you have room for is pain management. This is why we must all find a place of healing for our brokenness, because our souls need love to evolve.

Love and trust are inextricable. Without the capacity to trust, you can never really experience love. This is why the community of faith—and our experiences in it—are such an essential part of soul evolution.

But Do *I* Really Need This?

You might agree that for my mom (and others like her), trustworthy friends and a good church are important—even necessary. You can honestly rejoice about the role the Church can play in people's healing and restoration. This *is* a blessing! This *is* good! You really believe that and can genuinely celebrate it.

But maybe there are times where you can't help but wonder how all of this really matters to you and your life. You probably haven't been a POW. You readily acknowledge that lots of people have had to face challenges that are much more life-altering than anything you have had to face—so you honestly find yourself wondering how embracing and valuing community (as anything more than a new potential social network) matters to your own soul's evolution. You'd concede that it is important for people who really *need* it—but what if you are one of those who *don't* really need it?

There was a wealthy businessman who attended our church for many years. He was a self-made man. He was a smart and capable leader. He was also arrogant and narrow-minded. Stories circulated our city about his temper and his rudeness. Yet because of his wealth and status, he was rarely confronted. He was not particularly popular. He alienated friends and foes alike. He claimed to be a Christian. But his attitude and actions neutralized his effectiveness as an influence for Christ. He didn't have a horrible upbringing. He was not given to the abuse of drugs or alcohol (or so he said). He had children in the family business. They all went to church. But he didn't really *need* community—or so he thought.

You probably know people like this, and you also know how the story ends. In their senior years they become lonely and bitter people. To their face everyone smiles and tolerates them. But no one really respects them. No one wants to be like them—especially their kids—but somehow the kids can't seem to help themselves.

So here is the question I'd like you to consider: Who is more at risk of perpetuating the dysfunctions of their past—the person who has had to process extreme heartache or the person who has experienced mild trauma?

I think we'd all agree that our past experiences have (to some degree) shaped who we are today. Living around broken people—being raised by broken parents, growing up around broken siblings, being taught by broken teachers, being instructed by broken coaches, vacationing with broken relatives, and working for broken bosses in a culture that has broken values—has contributed substantially to our own brokenness.

However, we are not all broken to the same degree. We don't all have the same kind of "stuff" from our past to process. So let me come back to the original question, but ask it in a slightly different manner: Who is more likely to minimize the effect of their past— those who have had a really hard time or those who would describe their past as relatively normal?

When a person has had a hard past (encountering lots of brokenness), they usually know it—even if they have tried hard to stuff it. They see the depth of it eventually. When they do, no one has to convince them that what they saw or experienced was soul-destructive. As a result, they tend to be a bit more clued in to their need for healing. They more readily see the value and importance of community.

Conversely, when people look at their lives and they see it as relatively normal, they tend to discount their own need for healing. They look at the brokenness of the people around them—and the "mildly irritating" habits they have picked up as a result—and assume that because they didn't experience something traumatic, they are pretty much okay. As a result, they are much more likely to perpetuate the broken patterns of the past and underestimate their own need for community—and the help God intended for it to provide.

This is not simply a modern phenomenon. It goes all the way back to the time of Jesus. There was an occasion when Jesus was talking to a group of fairly religious people (not hypocrites, but genuinely "good" people). He was warning them about their own propensity to miss what He had come to establish. He was concerned that these "good people" would miss the benefits and healing of His way of life, because they were placing way too much confidence in their own capacity to "get it." To prod them, Jesus issued this warning:

> *"I tell you the truth, corrupt tax collectors and prostitutes will get into the Kingdom of God before you do . . . ."*
> Matthew 21:31, NLT

Why does Jesus say this? Is it because God has a thing for really *bad* sinners? I do not suspect so. The reality is that some people are more open to (and aware of) their need for healing.

This is actually one of the saddest parts of my own journey in community. I have watched people make the same mistakes over and over again—bemoaning their lack of willpower or blaming others for their inability to get over stuff. Yet when the suggestion is made to engage the power and help of community at some deeper level, I hear the same excuses over and over again. I really don't have time for *that*. Things aren't *that* bad. *That* is for people who have real problems. However, this isn't just about what we think we need—it is about understanding that community is foundational even to the nature of the God whom Christians worship.

One of the core Christian tenets is the proposition that our God is three in one—what we commonly refer to as the Trinity. G. W. Bromiley, in his essay on the Trinity in the *Evangelical Dictionary of Theology*, summarizes the doctrine by saying:

> Although not a Biblical term "the Trinity" has been found a convenient designation for the one God self-revealed in scripture as Father, Son and Holy Spirit. It signifies that within the one essence of the Godhead we have to distinguish three "persons" who are neither three gods on one side, nor three parts or modes of God on the other, but coequally and coeternally God.

In fact, this idea was so central to the thinking of the early Church that they held an ecumenical council at Nicea in 325 A.D., and these leaders created what we now refer to as the Nicene Creed, the one universally accepted creed across Christendom defining (as best we can with human language) the nature of our triune God.

Now, why does any of this matter? In short, it goes to something that Dr. Gilbert Bilezikian spent a lifetime espousing: "Community finds its essence and definition deep within the being of God . . . ."

Everything that we see (and even that which we cannot see) was created by a God who is in and of himself community. We are product of a God who lives in perpetual community; everything He does (and has ever done) is in the context of *we*. Can we honestly believe that we can do better on our own? The God of community calls us into community. If the God who has done everything beautiful has done so in community—why would we want do different?

Do we really want to assert that we know more than God?

The Challenge of Trust

So let's assume someone is willing to take another tentative step "into" community; they don't want to be arrogant. They don't want to act like they're smarter than God. Maybe you can identify with these feelings. The hesitation is real—and perhaps in your mind even justifiable. What's that about?

From early in our lives we are taught to be responsible for ourselves. We start life dependent on others for virtually everything. But in the normal course of human development (as we move through adolescence), we learn independence and self-reliance. This self-assertion is critical—though it is often a nightmare for parents to endure. Even so, healthy independence is a necessary precursor to eventual healthy interdependence. If we never learn what it means to be independent and responsible, we will never move beyond childish dependence. We'll never grow up. We'll never be good at relationship—with God or anyone else.

The problem we all face (to varying degrees) is that our first few forays into the world of interdependence don't always go so well. Other people's brokenness spills over onto us and messes with our world. As a result, many of us learn to live with a bias toward independence—for the sake of self-protection.. Our disappointing experiences in relationships eventually teach us not to trust others. When these negative experiences occur during our more formative years, the ill effect will be only that much harder to break.

As a result we face a serious dilemma. We need community, but we can't bring ourselves to trust it. Perhaps this is exacerbated exponentially around the Church, where there is an expectation for people to automatically trust their fellow Church members because they are "brothers and sisters in the Lord."

A fellow pastor, mentor, and longtime friend at our church has a little saying that I have found extremely helpful in this regard:

> As Christ-followers, we are quite enthusiastic and prolific in our advocacy of the benefits of our redemption (as we should—for it is incredible). However, we ignore the lingering effects of human brokenness to our own demise. Our brokenness is real. It remains real. Only heaven will ultimately fix it. —Dr. Rod Casey

What that means in practice (as we engage Christian community) is that trust ought to be extended slowly—even in the connection with fellow Christ-followers. Trust has to be earned. We don't automatically trust someone just because they know the right words. Trust is extended to the degree that integrity has been proven over time.

But even so, some of us have trouble trusting anyone—even when trust has been earned. Some of us have experienced pain so deep that we have vowed that we will never trust anyone ever again. Is that the challenge you face? Is this the one promise that you have actually kept? If so, I am going to invite you to consider breaking that promise and opening another door.

If you are hesitant, you are not alone!

Sometimes what keeps people from being willing to open this door is that people don't feel like they can trust themselves. They are not sure what integrity looks like, and whether or not they can accurately assess it. They need help in identifying the characteristics of trustworthy people. What does a trustworthy person act like?

1. *They are good listeners*—Their interest in you is genuine. They care about you as a person. Who you are and what you think about is important enough to discover and be taken seriously. Good listening skills are a hallmark of safer people.

2. *They keep confidences*—People worthy of your trust don't violate confidentiality—even as veiled "prayer requests." By

the way, if a person tells you someone else's secrets, they are probably sharing yours with others as well.

3. *They practice healthy boundaries*—Trustworthy people are people who aren't trying to "fix" you. They listen to you, pray for you, and will advise you (as you ask for it). But they don't own your problems, and they will give you the space to process them.

4. *They are slow to judge*—These people are aware of their own fallibility; they understand that everyone faces hardship. No one is perfect. They are not condescending or reactionary. They take failure in stride.

5. *They are able to say the hard thing*—People worthy of your trust know how to speak the truth in love. They don't just say what you want to hear. They are willing to appropriately risk saying something uncomfortable (with grace).

6. *They recognize their own limitations*—They know how to say "I don't know." They don't presume that they are the only people who can help. They are ready to include others (with your permission) in the healing process.

7. *They do what they say*—Trustworthy people are people who are faithful to their word. They are good about follow-through. If they promise you something, they keep their commitments. They are not given to excuse-making or blaming.

8. *They give you room*—People you can trust make space and extend grace. They understand that change is not easy and give you the time you need to figure things out. They respect your requests. They know how to be patient.

9. *They aren't put off by emotion*—They give you permission to cry, vent, and process your feelings. They are not inclined to edit or stifle your emotional processing. In fact, trustworthy people help you identify your feelings and explore what's behind them.

10. *They are ready to pray for you*—They don't just say they'll pray; they actually thoughtfully bring your needs before God. They comfortably pray with and for you. You feel at ease and sincerely cared for by their prayers.

These are the qualities we want to look for as we take the risk toward engaging community.

Better Than We Think

No eye has seen, no ear has heard, and no mind has imagined what God has prepared for those who love him. 1 Corinthians 2:9, NLT; see also Isaiah 64:4

One of the consistent themes of scripture is this idea that we simply don't know how good it can be. We are enamored with the crumbs that fall from the table, and God says, "I have prepared a feast for you to enjoy." We are entertained with the toys of trivialness, and God says, "I can introduce you to a kind of joy that fully satisfies and will give sustained life to your soul." We readily question the meaning and purpose of life, and God says, "Align yourself with what I am doing and you will never run short on a reason for being."

All this is true! But we just don't *see* it. It is even hard to imagine it. Why?

I suspect that much of it has to do with what we have become accustomed to and what we see as *normal* around us. Some of it has to do with how we define *good* and what is sold to us as that which we *should* long to experience. As a result, somewhere along the way we lose perspective. We learn to settle. We assume that to aspire to something more is an exercise in futility. Besides, what is more discouraging than dashed expectations?

What lifts us to a higher plane? Who reminds us that *this* isn't all there is? Where can we hear that we aren't crazy for needing something soul-satisfying?

The Church!

When community is functioning as God intended with gifted leaders leading us, inspired teachers teaching us, compassion-filled counselors pastoring us, creative artists provoking us, generous givers serving us—essentially each member doing their part—something supernatural *is* possible. Where the values and aspirations of Jesus are promoted as the most noble standard for living, things change. People change. We can begin to see what is possible. We see things differently. We can begin to experience the "life of the Kingdom" that Jesus spent so much of His time talking about.

Perhaps one of the biggest misconceptions out there about the Christian life is that the thrust of Jesus' teaching was simply to prepare us for another life in another place. We just need to hold on until Jesus comes back and that is when the real good stuff begins.

There is no doubt that heaven will be a wonderful place—no more crying, no more fear, no more pain, no more suffering—eternal bliss. Even so, when Jesus launched His earthly ministry, He was apt to use this phrase:

"The Kingdom of God is at hand . . ."

Essentially Jesus said that what He was proposing has benefit here and now. It is meant to prompt an evolution of your soul here on earth. It is not just about what is coming someday. It is for now! In that sense, the Church is a grand experiment. It becomes the place where we live this out. We become the people who dare to believe that *this* is actually possible. We inspire each other to see it. We encourage each other to believe it. We help each other to live it.

Yet it isn't just about gaining a new perspective on what is possible; it is also about gaining a realistic perspective on what is hindering the progress. In this sense, we are not just visionaries; we are also prophets.

Unfortunately, the image of the prophet and prophetic ministry carries with it such negative connotations in modern Church life. It typically includes the image of the blunt, ill-mannered, know-it-all type, pontificating on what everyone else needs to do to get things straightened out. Yet a careful study of the scripture endorses a very different picture. Note these critical qualifying passages:

We will speak the truth in love, growing in every way more and more like Christ, who is the head of his body, the church. Ephesians 4:15, NLT

So, if you think you are standing firm, be careful that you don't fall! 1 Corinthians 10:12, NIV

Humility and love are meant to govern the manner in which we deal with one another. It is characteristic of healthy community for people to be willing to speak truth to one another (even truth that may feel uncomfortable at the initial hearing of it). But the manner in which this is done is as important as the practice itself.

May God give us grace to go all the way there! May we give God permission to use community to transform us so that we might actually become what we dream about becoming—individually and corporately.

The Working of the Spirit

So let's come back to the real world. For the last few moments we have been dreaming and philosophizing about grand possibilities. This is critical, because it sets the tone, paints the picture, and defines the ultimate objective. Yet at some point we have to come back to the more pragmatic question: *Sounds great, but how?*

I wish I had a really straightforward answer to that question. But because we are fundamentally talking about the ways and workings of the Spirit, we are talking about a process that is full of mystery. And I am not saying that to avoid the question, it is simply the way it is.

The wind blows wherever it pleases. You hear its sound, but you cannot tell where it comes from or where it is going. So it is with everyone born of the Spirit. John 3:8, NIV

But here is something I think we can say with some measure of confidence.

God, for His own purposes (some of which we can speculate about, and some of which we must simply trust as His wisdom), works consistently in the context of community. He uses the community as His hands and feet, as His eyes and ears, as His voice in the world. But as essential as community is, community is not the ultimate agent of change. It is the Spirit of God who is the author of change. The community is a vessel the Spirit uses, but it is the Spirit who actually does the work. It may sound like a subtle difference, but it is a critical distinction.

It has been my experience that people tend to find it very difficult to maintain a sense of balance as it relates to community. We tend to make it too big or too small. We count on it too much or too little. It is everything or nothing. But what helps me in that process is to keep my eyes focused on the Author of all this good work. God, by the means of His Spirit, is the One inspiring growth and change. God is the One who is serendipitously at work behind the scenes to put us in touch with the right people at the right times. It is also the Spirit of God who actually produces the change within us as we cooperate with Him. And perhaps most surprisingly, He is the One who commissions and empowers us as difference-makers in a world that desperately needs us to be His community of grace-extenders.

Not long ago, I was sitting on a platform in a large auditorium, interviewing my mom. She was talking about her journey. She was full of grace and truth. She was sharing out of her pain, but the Spirit of God was using her to give hope to all who were gathered in the room. As I listened to her speak, I couldn't help but be reminded of what she was like when she was at her worst. I will never forget those days. I am sure she won't, either. But this person speaking to us on that day was not the same woman she once was. The Spirit of God has done a wonderful work. He used community—most notably some caring friends who lived around the block—to heal and redeem my mom's brokenness. There was no denying the beauty of the evolved soul who was sitting and sharing before us. In fact, God was revealing the strength of His healing power through this wounded healer—and for all who were willing to trust her story, a new chapter was opening for them as well.

LOVE

*People who realize that they are loved extraordinarily—love
extraordinarily.* —Pastor Rob Koke

My wife and I were eating dinner when the phone rang. When I answered the phone, I fully expected to hear a recorded voice giving me that once-in-a-lifetime "opportunity" to purchase some new siding for our home. Funny how they know exactly when we sit down to eat. I was ready with my snide remark. Surprisingly, when I answered, it was an actual human voice of a person we knew from church.

Admittedly, it was a gentleman that I didn't know very well. We'd had several conversations in the lobby, and he and his wife were certainly nice enough, but we weren't close friends. So I was a bit surprised when he asked if he and his wife could drop by. "Sure, why not?" was all I knew to say.

It struck me as odd when they pulled into our driveway, each driving separate cars. I assumed the worst. I assumed they were having some kind of marital challenge and they needed someone to talk to about it. Carol and I aren't professional marriage counselors, but we are good listeners and so people have always found it easy to confide in us.

When I answered the door, I was a bit taken aback by the couple's demeanor. This did not look like a couple in need of marriage counseling. They had broad smiles, and they seemed downright giddy. We invited them into the living room, but they said it would only take a minute.

I'm not sure my friend had thought through his little speech. He stumbled around a bit, but finally he said something like, "Well, my wife and I were praying about this, and we felt impressed to give this to you and Carol. We appreciate what you do for the college students. So this is our small way of saying thanks." In his hand he was holding out a set of car keys.

We were speechless.

I wasn't sure what to do. This kind of stuff happens only on TV or with/for really important people—not run-of-the-mill folks like us. Thing is, it was a really nice car, too. It was a beautiful Volvo. When I saw it, I couldn't hold back the tears.

But here is what really got me about that whole deal. This couple wasn't particularly well off. They could have made good money selling the car. So what is it that goes on in the mind of a person/couple that causes them to conclude, "Hey, let's give away this really nice car to a couple in our community who we know only moderately well, but who we think is doing something important"? How do people's souls expand to the point where they can do things like that?

It must be love!

And this is something that I have always appreciated about the Church. Even in my most irreligious days, I have always been impressed by the love. I remember when my mom was having some of her hardest times; people would come by to visit and pray for her. Others would bring meals for the family. When my sister had just come through a painful divorce, there were people in the Church who would secretly drop off groceries on her doorstep (at just the right time). A business owner who was only mildly acquainted with her situation helped her find a job.

The reason I was (and still am) so impressed by this is not just that people *do* these things, but that it actually *occurs* to them to do these kinds of things. I am ashamed to say I am usually way too self-absorbed for that. But my own soul is still evolving and expanding—thanks to the work of the Holy Spirit and the influence and help of the Christian community in my life. The more I realize how much I am loved by God and others, the more I actually think about loving. How can you not? How can it not affect what we say, what we do, and how we relate?

O Lord, help us all to do so more deeply!

The Final 10 Percent

I was sitting in a leadership conference and I heard about the practice of sharing the final 10 percent. The big idea is that when we are having conversation (most notably a difficult conversation), we tend to say only about 80 to 90 percent of what we are really thinking. We usually don't share the final 10 percent out of fear of being misunderstood. We don't want to hurt people's feelings. We don't want to appear harsh. We aren't sure how the other person will respond. So we hedge our bets. We withhold the final 10 percent.

This speaker was advising us that the Christian community ought to be strong enough to bear the weight of the final 10 percent (if we are willing to do it well—which goes back to that sharing-the-truth-in-love idea). His main point was that, contrary to popular belief, the benefits of this kind of candor far outweigh the risks.

Having engaged and endorsed this practice for some time myself, I can say with confidence that it is absolutely true. I have seen the benefits of this kind of candid interaction in every relational sphere of my life.

However, I have only recently begun to discover that sharing the final 10 percent has tremendous power when we're communicating something positive, too. In other words, as valuable as it is to be appropriately confrontational with the final 10 percent, there is an equal (if not greater) value in being appropriately complimentary with the final 10 percent. Perhaps that part sounds easy (who doesn't want to be kind?), but the truth is, we actually use all the same excuses on the complimentary side as well—*I don't want to be misunderstood. People will think I am weird. I'm not sure how others will take it.* Perhaps this is part of why Jesus made love a command:

> *"A new command I give you: Love one another. As I have loved you, so you must love one another."* John 13:34, NIV

This command always struck me as a tad odd at first. Who doesn't want to experience love? Isn't that the one thing there is just too little of—doesn't everybody agree that love is all we need?

As much as we would all agree that love is central and in fact the ultimate expression of goodness, you would think that this wouldn't need to be commanded. It almost seems in the same category as having to say: *"You must eat your ice cream!"* But no one has to say that. Ice cream is inherently good. I already know it is good. We all love it. In fact, if there is a command related to ice cream, it should be: *"Hey you, do not eat the whole half gallon in one sitting!"* And isn't a genuine experience with love infinitely better than even the best ice cream? So why didn't Jesus just say, "Try it, you'll like it!"

Is it perhaps because the notion of love (in our imagination) is more exciting and doable than its practice (in reality)?

As much as we value love conceptually, its practice is always risky. No matter what the expression of love (in word or deed), whenever you do it, you are putting yourself out there. You are making yourself vulnerable. It feels dangerous. You are never guaranteed a similar response in return. The truth is, we have a love/hate relationship with love.

I think Jesus understood this better than anyone. In fact, because He was always motivated by love, He probably wrestled with its practice every moment of His life. He knew that unless this was a nonnegotiable, we'd probably opt out more often than not. We might agree that something good can come from the expression, but we just hate feeling that vulnerable. So Jesus had to say it without reservation. This is to be *the* hallmark of My followers. The only way that the world will ever believe that our message has divine origin is if we love one another. I will go first. Then you follow Me.

There were about fifteen people in our living room. A young lady who had been in our church since high school was headed overseas to work with troubled teens in the U.K. It was something she had felt impressed to do for some time. The doors opened for her in a very serendipitous fashion. It was obvious that God had a hand in this. But the fact remained that she was going to be in a strange place among some very needy people. She had never really done anything like this before. She wrestled with feelings of inadequacy. What would she say? What if they didn't receive her? Would she be enough? Was this really the right decision?

On the night before she left, a group of her friends gathered together to encourage her and to love on her. We each brought a memento that would serve as a reminder to her that we would be praying for her and thinking about her. We read loving letters about the ways she had already touched our lives. We prayed sincere prayers, asking God to give her courage and strength for this new assignment. Tears were shed. We loved her freely. It was just the kind of reassurance she needed. At the end of the evening, I made a little speech about how this was not just *her* assignment. This was *our* assignment. We were going with her in spirit. Our friend doesn't come from a very healthy family situation. But we were certainly her "family" on that evening, and we got a taste of what the psalmist meant when he wrote:

How wonderful and pleasant it is when brothers live together in harmony! Psalm 133:1, NLT

Five months later, a group of us went to visit her. It was such a treat to see her with the kids. It was obvious that they were being touched by her love. What God helped us to impart to her the night before she left, she was now imparting to these young people. Love always feels like a risky thing to give, but its fruit is an amazing thing to behold. It *is* the gift that keeps on giving. I can see why

Jesus made it the main thing. Without it, nothing of significance ever happens.

But the empowering nature of love isn't just reserved for those on special assignment. It is actually designed to help "normal" people live their everyday lives.

My daughter served as a sales intern in Connecticut in the summer after her freshman year in college. The internship put her on thousands of doorsteps over the course of three months. In one particular phone conversation, she told me of a chance encounter that inspired and touched me.

She said, "Dad, meeting all these families has caused me to realize how good I have it. I have been so blessed by my family, friends, and faith. I have known such love in my life. In fact, I was thinking about that on the way to one house where I had been invited to make a presentation. When I got there, the son (a ninth grader) answered the door. He looked so down. I could hear his mother crying in the background. He said it wasn't a good time. He asked if I could come back later. In that moment I realized that making a sale was not the most important thing. I am not sure what came over me. I asked him if he would like a hug. He actually cried on my shoulder for a few moments. It was the coolest thing!"

First off, for those who don't know my daughter, this is quite out of character for her. She is kind, but also fairly reserved and private when it comes to physical touch. So for her to respond in that moment with that kind of sensitivity made a significant impression on me—and more importantly, on that ninth-grade boy. I know it is a seemingly small thing—just a hug—but isn't it often the smallest spontaneous expressions of care that can make the biggest difference in our lives?

I don't know what that young man was thinking as he stepped to the door that day. But I can imagine that for him it felt as though a fairly significant part of his world was falling apart. What was he going to do? He was probably feeling very much alone, wondering if anybody knew and anybody cared. As he went to answer the doorbell (at a most inopportune time), a kind college freshman was able to look beyond her own agenda to extend an expression of love that said most unexpectedly, "I care!" *Whoa!*

When you stop to think about it, isn't that the very thing that our world could use a little bit more of?

Drawing Lines

Ahhh, but this doesn't mean every attempt at love is automatically noble.

In my senior year in college, a seasoned Christian professor invited twelve of us to his home on Sunday nights. We were a group of young Christian leaders on campus. The professor was highly regarded, and we felt honored to be invited.

I think it was our third or fourth night we were together. We had just finished dinner. The routine was always similar. We'd come over around four thirty, hang out for a bit, have a simple snack dinner, and then discuss a subject of common interest regarding spiritual leadership.

In the previous weeks we had been talking about Christian community and how people can't give what they don't have. If our campus was to be touched by the love of Christ, then as Christian leaders we would need to learn to share that love freely with one another—so that from our positive community experience we would have something of substance to give away. Our love wouldn't just be theoretical. It would be real. We would be able to extend it—because we had experienced it. We were all very proud of our philosophizing. It seemed so right.

So on this particular week, our professor started our discussion with a very provocative question: "Tell me something. What are you going to do with your desire to sleep with one another?"

We were appalled. How could he even ask that kind of question? Didn't he know we were Christian leaders? I mean, really . . . I mean, dang, how did he know what we were thinking?

The point is that everything can be perverted—even love. It may not be the original intent. Good people can have noble aspirations, but given the brokenness that we live with and around, we ought not to be naïve.

genius of what my mentoring professor did for me that night is that he modeled the power of exposing secrets. Bringing light to the darker places protects us from our own foolishness. It encourages honesty and protects community. We do well to understand the challenge of creating and maintaining healthy community. The power of its testimony—when community is at its best—means that it is all the more susceptible to attack both from within and without. Wise participants recognize this inevitability and plan and act accordingly.

The tragic story that occurs repeatedly in Christian community is that it only takes one foolish decision (that often occurs in a moment of weakness) to destroy something good that took years to develop.

I have worked at this practice for over thirty years, and I am fully convinced that protecting community is not something that happens easily or by mere good intention. It requires constant vigilance. We are not naturally inclined to talk about the ways in which we are tempted to violate and compromise community. We prefer to keep that stuff hidden. But when it remains hidden, it only becomes more powerful.

Every community that hopes to survive as an authentic witness to the love of Christ must create its own self-protective strategy and declare it. *Here* is what we mean by community. *Here* is what that looks like. Therefore, *this* is how we will behave. *This* is what we are agreeing to. *This* is off limits. Then they talk about *it* a lot.

Sometimes people are afraid of talking about these things because it seems to assume the worst about others. But it is actually a matter of respect. It is an act of wisdom. It is dealing with reality. Talking about the hardship of sustaining healthy community honors the efforts of those who work diligently to protect it. It is a supreme act of love to acknowledge the discipline that great community requires. No one is above or more important than the community at large. So, young and old, leader and non-leader, experienced and inexperienced must be equally submitted to the good of the whole. This kind of proactivity affords us the rich benefit of what great community provides—while ensuring that its goodness can be sustained for as long as possible.

O God, You call us to be people who freely love one another. It is the thing You care most about. Yet we are inclined to pervert it—even when we taste the goodness of its purity. Make us wise. Strengthen our resolve to do this well, so that what this was meant to be may be what it actually becomes! By Your strength and power.

The Centrality of Forgiveness

People's experience with love—in any given community—is never the same. Some people seem to thrive and feel truly loved and accepted in certain places, while in those very same places others struggle.

Why is that? I think we have all heard the statement, "That is just *not* a very loving place. I never felt any love in that environment." However, others go to that very same place and are welcomed and embraced. How do we explain this?

Is it possible that environmental factors are not the only variables that affect one's experience in community? Is it possible that what we bring to the table individually impacts our experience as well?

I think so.

A longtime friend had been hurt as a girl in ways that are difficult to talk about. So she chose not to. What she did do was make a vow. She vowed that she would never allow anyone to get close enough to hurt her again. How do you think that vow affected her experience in community?

I don't like making all-inclusive declarative statements, but this is one I feel pretty confident about. I believe that the biggest impediment to people's experience in community is unforgiveness.

Unforgiveness poisons the soul. It insulates people from love. The very thing they most need in their lives becomes the very thing they won't give themselves permission to give or receive. Unforgiveness doesn't just affect the relationship between the offended and the offender—the accumulating bitterness eventually affects every relationship they have. Harboring resentment infects other relationships, because it warps one's perspective. It lowers trust. It creates suspicion. It breeds contempt against even the most undeserving people. The longer it festers, the bigger it gets. That is why unforgiveness becomes such a hindrance in the context of community. For the one who can't forgive, everyone in the community begins to look like the one not yet forgiven.

But it doesn't have to be this way. There is another path. We can learn to forgive, and forgiveness opens the door to the love we crave.

One of the reasons that people stay bound by their unforgiveness is because they have all kinds of misconceptions about what forgiveness actually involves. So before I describe its practice, let me clarify what it is not:

- Forgiveness does *not* mean that you excuse what happened.

- Forgiveness does *not* mean that there shouldn't be any consequences.

- Forgiveness does *not* mean that you will forget what took place.

- Forgiveness does *not* mean you turn off your feelings.

- Forgiveness does *not* mean the relationship is automatically restored.

- Forgiveness does *not* mean you don't learn from the experience.

- Forgiveness does *not* mean it's all okay now (and forever).

Rather, forgiveness is a decision to release your right to exact revenge. There is a lot behind that one statement, so let me play that out.

Forgiveness is first of all something we *decide* to do; it is not something we necessary *feel* like doing. Depending on the offense, forgiveness may actually be the last thing we feel like doing. Therefore, it is fundamentally an act of the will, and in many instances it is not something one can come to quickly. Some people even find it helpful to begin the process of forgiveness by praying this prayer, "Lord, please help me to be willing to be willing to forgive."

Again, to be clear, forgiveness is not the same thing as saying, "It's okay. It didn't really matter!" It is quite the opposite. Forgiveness begins with the acknowledgment that the offense was personally harmful. *This* hurt. *This* was not right. Therefore, you have a right to exact revenge, but instead of doing so, you release them to God to do as He sees fit. That is at the heart of what it means to forgive.

Jesus' prayer from the cross (where He forgives his executioners) is worth pondering. He says, "Father, forgive them . . ." (Luke 23:34, NLT). Note that He doesn't say, "Father, forgive them, because what they are doing isn't all that big a deal." Rather, Jesus says in effect, "They have no idea what they are doing—and what a big deal this really is! Even still, I entrust myself to You, My Father . . ."

So what should we expect to take place relationally—between ourselves and the one who hurt us? It depends on many different things:

. . . *the manner of the offense;*

. . . *the openness/repentance of the offender;*

. . . *the capacity and opportunity for trust-rebuilding;*

. . . *the effectiveness of and adherence to a reasonable process.*

But in many ways this is actually a secondary question. Don't let this issue get you sidetracked. The main concern is about what is happening in you. Remember, even though this involves another person (maybe even other people), forgiveness is about you first and foremost. Forgiveness is about how you respond to what happened to you. Forgiveness is about entrusting the outcome of the situation into God's capable hands.

When I speak on this topic in our church, I have to prepare myself for significant push-back. Sometimes people get very emotional about this subject. The assumption is that I am being callous and insensitive to the pain some people have experienced at the hands of cruel perpetrators. I get it! Believe it or not, I was in that very same place when my mother started talking about forgiving the people who abused her in the prison camp. I couldn't imagine her talking about—let alone attempting to do—any kind of "forgiving" of those who committed such heinous acts.

But my mom wouldn't let my unsettledness keep her from doing what she knew she needed to do. She knew she had to forgive her captors—and she was willing to do it for the sake of her own soul. She and I have had many conversations about her experience. She has taught me so much about what soul evolution looks like— especially with regard to the importance of forgiveness. Perhaps her learnings would be helpful to you as well.

There are three things that really stand out in my mind about what she taught me.

First, she repeatedly told me that people tend to underestimate how long this process takes—especially when people are dealing with something life-altering like abuse, or abandonment, or some other unexpected tragedy. We live in a world that wants things to be fixed quickly, and sometimes we are own worst enemies. One of the best things that a community of Christ-followers can do is to help strugglers be patient about the process. Let them talk it out. Let them voice their feelings. Provide perspective as appropriate, but never underestimate the power of your patience. Just sitting and being *with* them has such healing power—along with your prayers.

Second, she talked about having to revisit certain issues and situations repeatedly. There were times when she thought she had "let something go" but then a memory would resurface or she'd have another nightmare—and the emotions would get stirred up all over again. Forgiveness isn't typically something you do once and then you're done with it. It is a decision you make over and over again.

But that shouldn't surprise us. There are lots of things in life that are just like that. Marriage, parenting, friendships, business ownership (anything that matters to us) typically starts with a decision. We say to ourselves, *This is good. This is right. I am going to do this.* We know there are going to be hard days. When those days come, we remind ourselves why *this* is important and we decide to give ourselves to *it* again. Forgiveness works the same way. You decide to do it, and when it gets hard you remind yourself all over again why it's important, and with God's help you put one foot in front of the other and try and make it through another day.

Finally, she talked regularly about the importance of forgiving yourself. We often think forgiveness is just about what other people have done to us. But after we peel the layers back and get a good hard look at what is happening in our soul, we realize that there is much that is a mess "in there" because of things we have done to ourselves. "Ironically enough," she would say in that wise reflective voice, "we can know that God has forgiven us (read it right there in the Bible), but if we can't humble ourselves enough to forgive ourselves, we won't really experience the benefits of this forgiveness." In fact, for some this is the hardest part of all—to be humble enough to forgive yourself. Listen to my mom; she knows what she is talking about.

> *O God, the truth is, this runs deep. When Jesus taught His disciples how to pray, He linked our experience with forgiveness to our forgiveness of others (ourselves included). Help us to go there. May that place that has been locked away and set off limits, may the vows we have made in hurt and anger, may all that has bound us and robbed us of life and love, be broken. In Jesus' name!*

The Limitations of Love . . .

I was sitting in a counselor's office. I was coming through a particularly difficult season. There was something negative happening in almost every arena of my life—all at the same time. Individually, they weren't insurmountable problems, but together they had become debilitating. I was dealing with a series of personal losses that had begun to get the best of me. I was losing perspective and needed some wise counsel on how to process my next steps.

I am an idealist.

In many ways my idealism works for me. It motivates me to aim high and work hard. People say I am good at loving. As a result, people like being around me. People feed off my enthusiasm. But I often deal with disappointment. I wonder why things aren't better than they are. I often feel underappreciated and used by others.

After several sessions, I was challenged to face my expectations about life, love, and relationships. What I realized was that I have certain expectations about relationships that set me up for inevitable disappointment. Reality is just not that good!

Some people deal with the opposite problem. Some people are always waiting for the other shoe to drop. If something good happens, it will most certainly not last—and something really bad is sure to follow.

Christian community is a great thing. Real love can be known. Idealists and doomsdayers can help each other find redemptive perspective. In community all kinds of people experience love and healing. However, brokenness also remains. Community is not perfect. Community is not God. There are some things God alone can fix, and God doesn't fix everything in this life. Some things don't get fixed until heaven. How we react to that and how we process it determines an awful lot about the trajectory of the rest of our journey here on earth.

> *God, help us to fully appreciate (and enjoy) the benefits of what You have already made available to us in Christian community and grant us the grace to be patient in those places where we aren't fully satisfied. Give us the capacity to embrace the tension between the "already" and the "not yet" and the wisdom to know the difference.*

SERVE

In the early seventies I had an experience so powerful that it divided my life into before and after . . . I was a goner utterly captured by a single vision of the potential beauty of the local church. —Bill Hybels

Church life can be great—but it is also really hard. It is messy and complicated. Christians can be petty and immature. One week they can love their church. The next week they want to leave. Yes, soul evolution happens slowly and often reluctantly. You have probably heard (maybe even seen) some of this for yourself. But just in case you haven't, let me play out a conversation I have had on a pretty regular basis.

Let me introduce you to "Bob." Bob has been a part of our church community for three years. We have met for coffee before—quite often actually. Early on I invested fairly heavily in his spiritual journey. He had a lot of questions. Eventually he was baptized. I also walked him through a tough spell while his wife was battling breast cancer. But for the last three months I hadn't seen him as often—and I might be oversensitive—but it feels like he has been avoiding me. So instead of playing the guessing game, I decide to schedule a time to make sure everything is okay.

We arrive at the coffee shop around the same time. We grab our favorite spot in the corner by the back window that overlooks the creek that runs behind the shop. After exchanging a few pleasantries, I decide to dive right in.

"Thanks for meeting with me—it's been awhile."

"Yeah, no problem. You have always been so good to meet with me to help me with all my questions, the least I can do is return the favor."

"Well, I actually have a question for you this time. It's a bit personal. It may be a bit uncomfortable. But I'd like you to shoot straight with me. Deal?"

"Ummm, yeah, okay. I'm getting a bit nervous, but I'll do my best."

"We made an agreement when we started chatting that if we ever had a reason for concern, we'd extend each other the courtesy of being direct. We wouldn't go behind each other's back. We wouldn't talk to each other's friends. We wouldn't wonder in silence. We would just exercise some relational courage and have a candid conversation. I am glad we agreed to that, and I think we have developed the kind of trust where we can do that without putting the friendship at risk. Are you still in favor of that?"

"Absolutely, but with a buildup like that, you really have me curious."

"Well, the bottom line is that I need some help understanding what might be going on with you—and perhaps particularly with your involvement in our midweek ministry. I don't want to assume I know, because there may be things going on that I am not aware of—so I just thought I'd ask. What I have observed is that you haven't been coming as often. During our discussions you seem less engaged. When we did that project at the kids' home last weekend, you cancelled at the last minute. I am just wondering if there is something going on that we need to talk about."

<long pause>

"You know . . . I have wanted to talk to you about this for some time. I just didn't know how to bring it up. I was afraid you would take this personally—and it isn't personal. I was also concerned that you might think I was ungrateful for your investment. And I am extremely grateful. I don't even have the words to describe it. I mean, you remember where I was when we started our conversations. I was a mess!"

<long pause>

"Now I am beginning to feel really badly for not bringing this up earlier. But, here is the thing . . . I don't know . . . I have been doing a lot of thinking. Something is different. I remember when I first started going to the services, it was almost as though every talk was directed right to me. Every weekend was great! I met such cool people. I felt such love—that love you said was core to what it means to be a Christ-follower! I felt it. I was blessed by it. It was just as amazing as you promised."

"Then you invited me to this group, and it was so meaningful and helpful. The people were real. I was growing—a lot. But for the last few months I just haven't been feeling it. The sermons haven't been as meaningful. I really think there should be more references from the Bible. The music isn't connecting like it used to. I think the lead guy there is more about ego than worship. It's really starting to bug me. And my kids' soccer schedule is getting more intense—so it has just been harder to come to group."

"Wow, sounds like there really has been a lot going on . . ."

"Yeah, and here is the thing, I have a friend at work who has been bugging me to come to that new church at the corner of North and Vine. I went there last weekend. They have such an awesome kids' program. Their facilities are unbelievable. I am really starting to wonder if maybe I don't need something new to reignite my spiritual passion . . ."

<long pause>

The newspaper headline captured it this way: "Patron Pours Entire Pot of Coffee over Friend's Head!" Subtitle reads: "Yes, it was worth it!"

Every spiritual seeker I have ever known or worked with has had a season when it "just isn't working for them anymore," and the immediate assumption is that there is something wrong with the community. People become convinced that the community isn't doing what it should be doing—it worked for a while—but not anymore. Therefore, the only (logical?) alternative is to find another church community.

Let's pause here for a moment and see if we can't avoid being the brunt of a newspaper headline.

There are times when a "change in scenery" is necessary. People get transferred and move out of town. A scandalous sin compromises the integrity of the church's leadership, making it impossible to stay engaged in the community with a sincere heart. Perhaps there is a critical doctrinal issue that is altered by the denomination and the change violates one's conscience. The church mission and vision is unclear. No one knows what to do or where to go. Resources are being squandered, and despite numerous personal efforts to bring accountability and change, nothing happens. Life is too short to spend years swimming upstream, therefore a move has to be made. The Spirit of God may also prompt a change for reasons that are entirely personal. Things happen. There are legitimate reasons to transition out of a church community. Leave well. Don't gossip. Express appropriate gratitude.

But these legitimate departures seem to be more the exception to the rule. I am increasingly troubled by the haphazard "church hopping" that many Christians (western Christians in particular) are engaged in. People join and quit church for silly reasons. In fact, at the risk of overstating, it appears to me that the consumer mind-set regarding Church life seems like a sinister plot hatched by forces of darkness to keep people's souls from maturing.

So I would like to spend some time talking about what to expect once you decide to engage a faith community. I will touch on what makes it a meaningful experience and how the experience changes (and should change) as you mature in your faith.

In fact, if we were having this conversation face-to-face, I'd invite you to my favorite coffee spot, I'd grab a napkin and a Sharpie, and I would start drawing.

First, I'd draw a diagonal line from the left-hand bottom corner of the napkin toward the top right-hand corner. I'd say, "Let's let this line represent your spiritual journey. I realize our journey is never actually made with straight lines, because life is just not that predictable. But for the sake of discussion let's assume you have been making good progress. So the trend line is generally up and to the right."

Then I'd draw an oval circle all the way around the diagonal line and suggest that the oval represents the community that has been beneficial to you in your spiritual progress. The community was probably a part of your development long before you even knew about its existence—through the love and prayers expended on your behalf from afar.

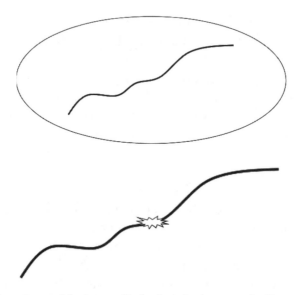

Then I would place a little "explosion symbol" somewhere in the middle of the line to represent a crisis moment (reflective of the kind of conversation I just had with Bob).

This crisis point is common to everyone—and the decisions that are made at this juncture are absolutely critical to the rest of the journey. You will get to this point, too, and when you do, it will be critical to walk through a series of questions—and take your time with them. Avoid a rash or emotional reaction.

Ask yourself: "Why am I here? What has contributed to my arriving at this place?"

Write down some of the more pressing concerns. Be honest. I can suggest a couple of the more common challenge points:

Weekend services just aren't as meaningful as they were before . . .

I often feel bored by the journey . . .

I just want to try something different . . .

People in the church bug me . . .

Spiritual pursuits have gotten harder to sustain . . .

Do you have a few of your own you'd like to add?

_____

_____

_____

_____

_____

In most instances the things that people put on their list are the more visible and obvious reasons for the feelings of unsettledness. They are worth considering seriously. But I am going to suggest that there may be something of greater spiritual significance stirring underneath it all. I wish someone had talked me through this when I experienced it for the first time. It might have spared me a few treks through the same learning turnstiles. Then again, maybe someone did try to warn me, but I wasn't all that interested in listening.

Is it any wonder Jesus was often quoted as saying, "He who has ears let him hear!"

Soul evolution has a rhythm often introduced by a season of unsettledness. We come to a place where we feel like something needs to change, but we are not always sure what to change. In fact, my experience is that we often misinterpret what needs to change. I certainly have. Paying attention to soul nudges isn't easy. But if we can learn how to interpret what is really taking place inside—and make the right connections—something truly life-changing can happen.

When we feel unsettled (in this season), our knee-jerk reaction is to assume that there must be something wrong "out there" in the community. When we feel some disequilibrium we figure there has to be a tangible reason for it, so we tend to *blame* it on something we're convinced is "no longer working" in our circumstances. *This* is what is causing the discomfort. The preacher isn't biblical enough. The leadership is too dogmatic. The music has gotten louder. The people aren't as nice as they used to be. I just don't feel right about the youth program.

This is *why* I feel unsettled.

Conveniently, if our assumption is that the internal stirring is a product of an external problem, it doesn't take much effort to actually find something "wrong" to justify that suspicion. There is always something wrong, isn't there?

I am convinced this is what lies behind much of today's "church hopping." This is why people are so willing to switch to a new community—the new community with the better preacher, the hotter band, the newer facilities, and the more popular youth program.

The assumption is that if we can change what is *wrong* in the community (by finding a better one), then we will no longer feel unsettled. But, amazingly, it isn't long before the unsettledness returns in the *new* community! This time it is because the pastors are not accessible enough, the governance is too stringent, and the doctrine is too narrow.

No wonder people are bailing on the Church left and right. The Church is such a mess!

Or maybe that's not the issue at all!

Maybe it is just time to consider the dynamic of unsettledness from a totally different angle. What if the sense that "something isn't exactly right" has *nothing* to do with the imperfections of our community? What if the unsettledness is God's way of gaining my attention about the fact that something has to change in *me*? Maybe the whole reason I/you feel unsettled is because our souls realize that it is time for another step in evolutionary process. The soul is unsettled over its own need for growth. Therefore, it has very little to do with what is happening "out there" and has everything to do with what has to change "in here."

The reason the soul gets unsettled is because it is ready for something more. But how do we know what the soul needs? Critical question!

Let's go back to the napkin and the little "explosion point" we made on the line. I am going to suggest that almost all the soul development that occurred to the left of the crisis point was a product of what the community invested in you. The community existed for your benefit. You were a consumer of ministry. You were the beneficiary of community. This is typical.

THE COMMUNITY EXISTS FOR YOUR BENEFIT.

The crisis your unsettled soul is hinting at now is related to the fact that you have come to a new season in the context of community. The community no longer exists simply for your benefit; you (increasingly) exist to add value to the community. Your soul is actually longing to figure out what it has to contribute. It wants to know and go—hence, unsettledness!

In fact, I contend that much of your soul's growth from this point forward will come in the midst of your making your contribution in the community. This doesn't mean that the community won't provide spiritual support and encouragement. Of course it will. But your new growth edge (for the foreseeable future) is about understanding and fulfilling your own call within the community. Your growth will come as much from what you give as from what you receive.

YOU EXIST FOR THE COMMUNITY'S BENEFIT.

Called to Serve—And Living It

Jesus was notorious for saying things that didn't seem true on the surface. At first blush, you are tempted to think, *That can't be true.* But as you live them out, you discover they are in fact true.

This is actually where faith plays such a huge role in the journey. Faith is required when certain actions contain rewards that aren't readily apparent. Faith takes action on things that the mind doesn't appreciate until later. One of these faith-required counterintuitive statements of Jesus is:

"It is more blessed to give than to receive." Acts 20:35, NIV

To be on the receiving end of something really good sounds like the best deal out there—at least initially. I'm sure you have been the recipient of a thoughtful gift or an unexpected kindness. That is pretty nice. Hard to beat. Unless you are the one who actually gives the thoughtful gift or extends the unexpected kindness. That really does feel more blessed.

In the same way, it would seem like the best deal going is to be served by a gifted (yet humble) person who loves sharing something with you that is personally rewarding and meaningful. That is pretty cool—really cool actually. But to be the person who can do that kind of thing for others is even better.

That is what Jesus espoused. But He didn't just talk about it; it was the dominant theme of His life.

"Just as the Son of Man did not come to be served, but to serve, and to give his life as a ransom for many." Matthew 20:28, NIV

"Greater love has no one than this, that he lay down his life for his friends." John 15:13, NIV

This was Jesus' life. And what is so striking about what He did is that He did it with such joy. This wasn't obligatory. His service wasn't born out of religious duty. This was His preferred way of living. He was convinced that this is the best kind of life. His invitation to join Him—which is still calling to us through the centuries—invites us to continue this countercultural way of doing life. He says: *Discover the joy in serving!* Now, this is not an easy kind of life. It is hard. But it's the good kind of hard.

I remember when I first started hearing about this idea of service as the "big deal" in following Christ, my initial assumption was that whatever I would be asked to do would be something I would hate. I am not sure where I picked this up, but for some reason I had equated distasteful assignments with spiritual commendations. So the more I didn't like doing something, the happier God would be with me—as I did it.

And candidly, serving always requires that we be willing to lay down our sense of entitlement. There are so many times where even maturing Christians think that they ought to have this or that, or that they are beyond such and the other. But adopting the spirit of service is all about dying to that sense of "I'm past *that.*" I believe this is fundamentally what Jesus meant when He talked about our taking up our cross to follow Him. It means we are willing to deny ourselves. But the unexpected joy is that when we take the low road and when we are willing to say "Your way is better than my way," our souls are brought to life in ways we never expected.

> No man or woman is an island. To exist just for yourself is meaningless. You can achieve the most satisfaction when you feel related to some greater purpose in life, something greater than yourself. —Denise Waitley

In short, if you want to know life—as it was meant to be lived— then lay down your agenda and join in with what God is doing in and through His family (the Church). When you do that, you will discover a kind of life that is beyond what you thought possible.

Again this doesn't seem like this would be right. How could dying to your own ideas and embracing God's higher purposes be better for you? You might see how it is better for God—but how can this actually be better for you? Is it possible that there is something inside of you (part of your hard-wiring) that longs to know this kind of self-sacrificial joy—a secret your soul is longing for you to discover, but which is not yet clear to you?

Consider the tastiness of a chocolate truffle. Wait . . . What? Hang with me. When you look at a truffle, it looks like a rather ordinary piece of chocolate. It doesn't give you much of clue that there is something truly wonderful inside. Maybe the size is a hint, but other than that, it looks innocent. Understated. In fact, if you have never eaten a truffle you would have to take it on faith that there is more than meets the eye. But . . . Oh my . . . After the first bite, you realize this is not your ordinary piece of chocolate.

French chocolatiers reserve their finest and most exquisite ingredients for the inside of their chocolate masterpieces—and they relish the mystery and surprise of what can be hidden inside. The point is that after you have tasted some of these delightful creations, you start wondering why you ever settled for bland, boring plain chocolate for so long! This is exactly the same response so many people have when they begin to make a connection to God's purpose for their own lives. Why did I wait so long to serve? Why did I settle for plain boring chocolate when I could have had a truffle?

Serving God in the context of your local church can become the most thrilling part of your life!

Embracing the Community's Agenda

Before I leave this matter of finding and fulfilling our sense of calling through service in and to the community, we also need to consider the interaction between one's personal assignment and the broader calling of the corporate community.

In one of his first books, which is still a personal favorite of mine, *Developing the Leader Within You*, John Maxwell underscores the importance of community members paying close attention to the vision and values of the larger community. He accurately observes that those who sincerely and proactively align their serving to help the community achieve its greater mission are the ones who end up finding the greatest amount of affirmation and satisfaction in their roles of service.

The reason this has relevance is because many potential ministry activists (who are personally excited about serving), often miss the fact that there is a broader overarching corporate mission that rightfully governs ministry priorities. Therefore it is incumbent upon every serving member to have a dual sensitivity both to their own personal responsibilities and the overall purposes of the Church. Those who miss this connection or ignore this dual sensitivity invariably get frustrated, because their contributions often seem unappreciated or undervalued. They often feel like they remain on the outside looking in—even as they claim to be ready to do their part.

The resistance they feel is not usually a result of any lack of sincerity or skill with regard to the service they are offering. Rather, it is likely that leaders can sense that the one offering the service may have an agenda that is at odds with the thrust of the community's mission. Those charged with leading the community often have an innate intuition about these kinds of inconsistencies and will lean toward protecting the community's vision and values—as opposed to risking mission confusion by accommodating multiple personal agendas.

This is the leader's responsibility!

And yes, it is all that complex. Might as well be candid about that right up front. If it were easy, anyone could do it. Perhaps that is why it is helpful to remember that this is ultimately the Lord's work—the Lord himself is building His Church.

Unless the LORD builds the house, its builders labor in vain.
Psalm 127:1, NIV

OWN

I no longer call you servants, because a servant does not know his master's business. Instead, I have called you friends, for everything that I learned from my Father I have made known to you. John 15:15

There were two hundred people gathered in the auditorium for a leadership event. There was great food, meaningful conversation, and a bold and compelling vision shared about the future of our church. It was one of those great "feel good" events where everybody left fired up about the future. Only one problem, as everyone was leaving, the toilets throughout the building started backing up. Now people weren't feeling so great about the future.

Our church hosts a Saturday evening service, so in a matter of hours the building would be full of people again—and finding a plumber on such short notice would be no small miracle.

Without any fanfare, three guys who were in the meeting and had heard about what happened said, "We'll take care of it." They diagnosed the problem and went to the hardware store. They bought the parts with their own money and made the needed repairs. They spent their precious Saturday afternoon fixing toilets—and that was after having already spent the whole morning at the leadership event. I am just guessing, but I suspect they actually had something much more exciting planned for that Saturday afternoon.

What struck me about what they did was how *normal* this all seemed to them. They weren't looking for attention. They didn't ask for their names to put in the program. I only found out about it because someone on the maintenance staff happened to mention it to me. But for the guys who did the work (sacrificing the most favored time of the week), this was just what committed people do. What else would you expect?

Their comment when asked about it, "This is *our* church!"

They instinctively understood it was their church. Not the pastor's church or their family's church. It was *their* building. It was *their* community. They saw themselves as highly invested.

"Our" Church

Words mean things. Language matters. The words people choose reflect their mind-set.

The word *our* is a word of ownership and identity. It acknowledges the fact that the community (and our experiences in it) is a joint effort, and each member carries real and personal responsibility for its health and longevity. Owners know this and use the language that reflects it. This is *our* job.

It is subtle distinction—but it is significant. Once you know to look for it, you can hear it everywhere. It is revealed in a simple passing comment. It is shared after a special event or service. Someone will be reflecting on what happened, and they will comment on the experience by saying one of two things:

What could our *church have done about that?*

Or...

It was their *responsibility to do something about that!*

Both statements sound similar. Both comments can be sincerely expressed. The difference is simply one word—*our* versus *their.* But that one word makes a world of difference.

So long as this is about what *they* do, then the community's vitality is someone else's responsibility. A person may see themselves as a contributor on some level, but they are not really responsible for the whole until they begin sincerely using the words *mine/our* as they reference the community. This move from *their* to *our* is a critical shift.

Joining the Church

Culturally we are increasingly "non-joiners"—just ask your local Lions Club or Rotary Club president. We don't mind helping; just don't ask us to become members!

As a result, it is possible that you also feel some resistance to the suggestion of "joining" your church community. But before you start practicing your internal back-stroke let me remind you of what you are being invited to consider. Remember the clarification in the interlude about the Church. It is not the building. It isn't the institution. It's not the weekend experiences. It's the community. It is people moving together toward a particular mission—growing and serving one another in an effort to share and reflect the love and message of Christ to one another.

Can you join *that*?

What do I mean when I use the word *join*. Do I mean that a person has to go through a formal membership process at a church? Is our participation not legitimate until we have physically signed on some dotted line? I'd like to speak with some boldness on this matter. I think there is way too much irrational reaction against systems and structures in our day. They are not the enemy.

I will often hear people say things like, "I am all for being spiritually minded and even God-directed, but I am just not into organized religion." I am often tempted to come back with the smartass reply, "Well, would you prefer disorganized religion?" But I realize that is probably not a very pastoral thing to say.

But consider this: It is a reasonable—and I would suggest even necessary—thing for those who are charged with leading a diverse community to create systems and structures that protect the community. Creating a process that helps people identify (and declare) where they are in their own personal development is helpful to the community. Having a procedure that insures that those who have influence within the community are qualified (and proven) to exert their influence in a way that is consistent with the mission and values of the community is equally essential. These are not just matters of efficiency and bureaucracy; it is a matter of faithful stewardship. In fact *not* creating the processes that help facilitate these opportunities for personal declaration and identification would be negligent and irresponsible given the weight the Church has been asked to carry for the sake of the Gospel.

I did say I would be bold.

Let me see if I can't raise the squirm factor one more notch. I think we *all* need this. These processes aren't just *good* for the community. They are *good* for us. It is good for the soul to submit and declare.

Let's go back to the baptism experiences I discussed earlier in the book. Why is that such a powerful experience for so many? I suggested that it had something to do with the power of declaration. Baptism is one's personal declaration. Joining the Church is one's corporate declaration. Our soul evolves as it declares. Our soul gains strength as it moves toward a humble but deliberate identification with a community. The idea is that pride-busting experiences can be great soul-building experiences. Jesus identified it as the mystery of losing one's life in order to gain it:

> *"Whoever finds his life will lose it, and whoever loses his life for my sake will find it."* Matthew 10:39, NIV

In other words, it's more than just an administrative detail to walk through a membership process at your church.

Even if you were Mr./Ms. leadership person in your last community, should God bring you into a new place among a new group, to serve and be served, there is no shame in saying, "I can submit to this process. I will earn trust. It will be good for my soul." In fact, might you imagine yourself saying, "I will thank God for the joy of connecting to a community that is fortunate enough to be led by leaders who believe that *this* is actually an important enough fellowship to protect"?

How is that for an attitude to aspire to?

The Heart Will Follow

As important as any "joining exercise" might be, I think we all know that because we are talking about soul evolution, there is always a deeper and more foundational connecting point. Sometimes those points are hard to figure out—which is why we might need to ask someone a little higher on the spiritual food chain.

Very few people like coming to a pastor for the very first time. In some people's minds, going to see the pastor is like going to see the principal. However, as every other conceivable resource has been exhausted—and not worked—some people might eventually make an appointment with the big dog.

The scene often unfolds in the same way. The first visit is the hardest, and the conversation often sounds something like this:

"Thank you for seeing me. I know you are busy, and I don't really want to take much of your time."

<all the while rubbing their hands together, trying to figure out where to sit>

"Well, here is the thing. I have been coming to the weekend services for a while now. I really appreciate what I am learning. I am growing in ways that I had never imagined possible. So I have wanted to get more involved. I went to Newcomer's class. That was good. I have also tried a couple of the groups, and they have been pretty good. Everybody is really nice. I have even started volunteering as a greeter. That's been good. But . . ."

<long pause>

"But I still don't "feel" connected. I don't really feel like this is "my" church. It seems like a place I come to—to get some spiritual nourishment. But I keep thinking there has to be more to it. I just can't figure out what I am missing, and I was hoping you might be able to help me."

"It sounds like you are paying attention to the unsettledness inside. That's a great important first step. You are getting helpful information at the weekend events. You are apparently reflecting on that information and taking it seriously. You are also giving back in a way that is meaningful. All that is good. It also sounds like you want to make this your community—and you are ready to take the next step in that journey. Is that right?"

"That is exactly right!"

"Okay, well, let me bring up an uncomfortable subject. I'm asking you to trust my heart on this. I want to answer honestly the question you are asking—and sometimes in soul matters that requires addressing the more uncomfortable questions (that we tend to avoid unless we are asked directly). So, let me ask, have you begun to participate financially?"

<long pause>

Apparently, there are surveys out there that suggest that one of the biggest hurdles to people's participation in the life of the Church is the critique that "the Church" is always talking about money. In fact, it is made to sound as though every reference made to money at church invariably brings rolling of the eyes and the insatiable urge to turn and run out of the building. I always find this humorous—and a bit puzzling.

My wife and I were invited to a fundraising event, where monies were being collected to support a new private school initiative. The whole event was about removing as much money as possible from every attendee's wallet or purse. That was the not-so-subtly *stated* objective. The whole town showed up—at least all the money-people. Everyone had a wonderful time bidding on items for sale and giving their money away. There was plenty of ribbing going on about how "ol' so-and-so" was being a cheapskate for not being more generous. Several hundred thousand dollars were collected that night. I suspect they will all be back next year. It seemed to me lots of people enjoyed the experience of giving generously to a cause they believed in.

People do seem to love giving generously to things they believe in. The Church and its mission merit support as well. It makes sense. It *is* good—again, not just for the recipients, but for the participants as well. Now obviously there are exceptions to the rule. We are all aware of the shady television evangelist who pilfers the pockets of the poor, and I agree with Milton that there is probably special place in hell for those who take advantage of the widow and the orphan.

But I'm convinced that these are the exceptions to the rule. In many congregations, a lot of pastors (if not most) shy away from talking about money—often out of fear that they will be accused of *always* talking about money. The irony is that Jesus (whom many hold as the epitome of spiritual sensitivity) talked an awful lot about it.

So in the spirit of Jesus, let's discuss finances for a page or two.

What we do with our finances is one of the biggest battles of the soul. There is something about money that makes it a prime place for spiritual wrestling. It has to do with power and independence. When people have money they have options. They can *make* things happen. People can feel like God. It becomes intoxicating. I think this is why Jesus made it such a point of demarcation. He said you can't serve money and God—because invariably money will become your God (see Matthew 6:24). Conversely, a lot of great soul evolution can happen as we resist this kind of idolatry and learn how to make biblical money management an expression of worship to the one true God.

With that in mind, I'd like to focus on three themes that Jesus reiterates with amazing regularity in His teaching on money. The first is the foundation, and that is that our use and approach to finances is a telltale sign of the condition and strength of our soul. Jesus said it this way:

"For where your treasure is, there your heart will be also."
Luke 12:34, NIV

We can't escape it. Follow the money. Where our money is, there our soul will be also. I think the implications of this are significant. If we are saying with our mouths that our community of faith is one of the most important parts of our lives, but little (if any) of our financial resources are being invested there, we are being disingenuous at best.

Conversely, if we are making priority-grade financial investments in the community, we might be amazed at how much a part of it we begin to feel. We realize in ever-increasing ways that what we give really does have a positive net effect on the overall health of the community. It sounds simplistic to say, but it's so true: If you want to feel more connected to the community, give more of your money to help ensure its success.

The second main theme in Jesus' teaching is that we all have differing levels of responsibility. The ones who have been entrusted with greater capacity are the ones who bear greater responsibility. Jesus put it very simply:

"From everyone who has been given much, much will be demanded." Luke 12:48, NIV

This may be one of the main reasons that there are so many biblical cautions about our aggressiveness in pursuing financial success. There isn't anything inherently wrong with money. Money is not the root of all evil (as oft misquoted). It is the *love* of money that wreaks havoc on the soul (1 Timothy 6:10); the reason being that accumulating lots of money caries with it an immense responsibility and high accountability. In our culture the temptation is strong (even blatantly advocated) to see this money as *our* money.

The truth, however, is that everything we have is a gracious gift of God. He gave us the capacity to think and work—in order to earn it. He opened the doors to create an opportunity for us to multiply it. He has allowed us to live in a time that grants us the freedom to pursue it. The lie that is perpetuated (and that many people instinctively believe) is that anything can be seen as legitimately *ours*. It is not ours. It is His. He entrusts us as managers, and there is a day of reckoning coming to the Owner of it all.

Every time my wife and I review our budget, we see our discussion on giving as our most important antidote against self-absorption. Every time we write a check to support the church, or a building project, or a missionary, or some other Christian cause, we see it as our personal proactive vote against materialism. It feeds the soul and starves the selfish side of us every time we do so. It reminds us that *this* isn't ours. This is all His and we do well to remember that to whom much entrusted much will be required.

Finally, Jesus also talked often about the fact that generosity will be supernaturally rewarded. Unfortunately, some people will insist on denigrating this incredible life-giving truth to some cheap formulaic theologically justified get-rich-quick scheme. How tragic! I believe the thrust of Jesus' whole discussion on the blessings associated with generosity has to do with the joy of being considered trustworthy.

> *"Give, and it will be given to you. A good measure, pressed down, shaken together and running over, will be poured into your lap. For with the measure you use, it will be measured to you."* Luke 6:38, NIV

This is a powerful, awe-inspiring promise, the gist of which is that you can't out-give God. Let's pause for a moment and consider the heart of what God is attempting to teach us. It wouldn't make much sense for God to "spoil people" with an increase in financial blessing, if it simply meant that they can now squander the increase on materialistic pleasures. How would that further His purposes? What does make sense—and certainly seems more consistent with the overall theme of Christ's radical form of discipleship—is to see this promise in the light of trustworthy stewardship.

If a person has been blessed by God with an increase in financial resources and the person blessed with these resources makes a practice of sharing generously—with greater joy and faithfulness with each progressive blessing—then yes, God loves granting the increase. He even arranges it!

This practice has amazing soul-expanding properties. I remember when I was challenged to see it this way early on in my faith journey.

It was a beautiful Saturday morning in my senior year of college; there were five to six of us sitting at a coffee shop. We were talking about what we were going to do after graduation. A professor who had joined us asked us to dream a bit about our future. As we were going around the circle each person talked about noble ministry-oriented dreams. One of us was going to start a church. Another was going to start a center for troubled youth. Another was going to be a missionary to a foreign country. And so it went. It almost sounded like the spiritualized version of "Can you top this?"

When we were done talking, my professor asked a very simple (but important) question. "So which of you is going to be the successful businessperson, because somebody is going to have to fund all this stuff?"

Around the Church, we can make it sound like the only really spiritual professions are those related to vocational ministry. Add to that all the talk about the evils of money and it can almost sound as though the person with any kind of business skill (and gifted with the capacity to earn wealth) is the poor stepchild—relegated to looking through the community window from the outside in. But their contribution has just as much value (when motivated by an evolving soul) as any other person's contribution.

Candidly, many Christian communities don't really know what to do with people of means. People of means don't always know how to relate to Christian communities. No one wants to show favoritism. We gladly applaud our musicians, but we ignore the businessperson—except when there is a building program (then we hope they'll take a "leadership" position). Granted, it *is* complicated. But maturing communities learn how to talk to each other about these complexities. No one gift is exalted above another—and no gift is ignored. Each part does its work—so that the whole community benefits and builds itself up in love.

A Crazy Kind of Love

In reading back over what I just wrote, I can imagine that there are some who have walked through this material thinking: *You see, this is exactly what I thought—at the end of the day its all about the stuff you have to do. It's all about being committed to people you don't really like, doing stuff that isn't really fun, and feeling guilty if you aren't giving large portions of your money to charitable causes!*

If you feel that, I appreciate your candor and understand your skepticism, but I also want to speak with the voice of experience and assure you that when this is a deep work of the soul, it's totally different. It really is!

For example, in order to write this manuscript, the leadership of the church community I serve graciously released me to write a book they thought might have value in the larger community of Christ. They did so willingly and joyfully—even though my absence as the senior leader created some complications for them in that they had to find guest speakers and carry a larger leadership responsibility themselves while I was writing. In a way they were thinking about you without even knowing you by letting me take the time to write this for you. And again, they did so with joy!

That is just the beginning. In the last thirty days (and I wouldn't say this is an unusual run), I have had numerous personal experiences with what might be considered "crazy" expressions of love and commitment. These actions illustrate the hard soul work I have just described, but more impressively, the sheer joy of living this out.

The day before I left town, I hugged the neck of a young man who over the last few years had become active serving as a spiritual coach to many men in our church. In the course of serving, he increasingly sensed that the Lord was calling him into vocational ministry. This would mean a huge shift in his life—and not just for him, but for his wife and three little girls as well. He sold his ownership interests in his insurance business, put his beautiful home on the market, and joyfully released his meticulously maintained BMW. He was headed off to seminary. After hugging his neck and looking in his eyes, I didn't notice reluctance or regret. Rather, I saw excitement for an adventure he couldn't wait to explore.

In my first week of writing, I got an e-mail from a businessman in our church. He had been in the service the previous Sunday and was encouraged by the words that he heard. In fact it was amazingly congruent with a book he had read not long ago that had a huge impact on his life. So he wrote me to ask if it would be okay if he bought that book for our congregation—one per family. He thought it might make for a nice tie-in to the series, and maybe someone would be blessed by the resource in the same way he had been. We have a large church community, so purchasing a book for every attending family would mean eight hundred books! When I wrote him back to thank him for his generosity, he simply said what he always says when he does this kind of thing (this is the third time he has purchased books for our congregation). "Piet, as always, please keep this anonymous. I have been blessed by God in amazing ways. I love giving back, and this is one small way where I can make a contribution and I love doing so."

There is a dear couple in our church who drive a little over two and half hours every weekend they are in town to join our community for our worship experiences. They love our church. Just before I left to begin my writing project, they took my wife and me out for dinner and said, "We really believe in what you are doing. We think you have a writing gift, and we just want you to know we have created a little fund that you can access to help cover some of expenses associated with getting this published." They don't want credit—probably are uncomfortable with my even putting anything about it in the book—they just did it because they feel so blessed to be where they are and love giving back in ways that seem right in the moment.

Last week, I had an extended phone call with an attorney friend of mine who volunteered to help me edit the book. He is great with language and grammar and clarity of communication. I was talking to him about compensation, and he said, "Listen, Piet, I appreciate you thinking about that—and if the book is wildly successful we can talk more about it. But you have to understand, this is a joy for me. I love doing this. I am glad you're willing to trust me with it. Let's just do something great together." Did I mention that he is a really busy guy with lots of responsibility in his other life?

And it isn't just the "big" things.

Every day while I have been away, my publicist has written me a short note to encourage me in my writing. Three days ago I received an e-mail from a prominent businesswoman who shared excitedly about her opportunity to talk to two hundred Girl Scouts about her work among AIDS orphans in Malawi. I had lunch last week with old friends from college who were getting ready to spend a week in Brazil (at their own expense) to encourage indigenous leaders of churches they planted fifteen years ago. Last night, my wife and I went out to a wonderful restaurant, because some friends from home said, "Hey, you gotta do more than work up there. We know a great place to eat. Enjoy a great meal, our treat!" We met a delightful couple at the church we visited this past weekend. They promptly invited us over for dinner and we became fast friends.

I could go on.

The point being, in each and every case, these acts of sacrificial kindness and love had no hint of obligation or begrudging duty. Rather, each expression was an enthusiastic, joy-filled act of love of a different kind—a little crazy. It is the love of souls that are full and that know of no other way to live. For it is the life they have always wanted! Should you be willing to engage the process for yourself, you might just find the same to be true for you.

Your soul is rooting for you to do so . . . .

EXTEND

Preach the gospel at all times, if necessary use words . . .
—Saint Francis of Assisi

According to Aesop's fable, a farmer and his wife found a goose that could lay a golden egg. It laid one golden egg each day, and as you can imagine, the couple was elated to discover this wonderful freak of nature.

Unfortunately, as the fable plays out, the couple eventually becomes greedy. They weren't getting rich quickly enough—and assuming that the inside of the goose was made entirely of gold, they killed the goose, only to discover that the innards were like any other bird. As a result they lost the very means by which they gained their wealth.

Good fables stand the test of time because they make an enduring point, a life lesson that has application across time and across cultures. What is the point of this fable?

We might suggest that it has something to say about being grateful for what you have. It is a caution against greed. All of this is true. But let me add a slight twist to the story.

What if the couple that discovered the goose were serious Christ-followers? Would we expect them to have treated the goose differently?

We would suspect so

We might expect that they would be grateful for their provision, thanking God for His unusual extension of grace. This would most certainly have affected their treatment of the goose. But, in addition, we would probably also expect them to share the eggs. We would expect the couple to joyfully share from their unexpected wealth. They should gladly give out of what they had so undeservedly received. We would expect this because even if we don't know a lot about what Jesus said specifically, we do know enough to know that Christian people should be generous. If they are not, even the culture critiques the hypocrisy. And they are right in doing so, because Jesus did say:

"Freely you have received, freely give." Matthew 10:8, NIV

It seems obvious! When someone has received an undeserved gift that makes one's life richer and continues to do so—that bounty *ought* to be shared! To not do so would be antithetical to everything that Jesus taught.

But an interesting thing happens when you try and talk about faith. A Christ-follower genuinely feels as though he or she has just found the goose that lays the golden egg (for their soul). Their life is immensely richer. In addition, the grace that has been experienced is so much more than a single life-giving encounter. It is literally the gift that keeps on giving. Therefore, how can it not be shared?

The problem is that we live in a pluralistic culture that sees sharing one's faith as anything but a generous act. It is called many derogatory things—proselytizing, pushing beliefs, being on the God squad, and some might even refer to it as "hate speech."

So for Christ-followers who are attempting to be generous with the gift entrusted to them in a culture that can see such action as hate speech, significant resistance exists. In fact, I am not even sure how to proceed from this point myself. As a reader you may have a budding commitment to share your faith and you want to figure out how to avoid the cultural landmines. Or you might not yet be fully convinced about the claims of Christ yourself and the very thought of having to talk about any of this has a pretty high cringe-factor.

So let me speak from a personal perspective and share about the kind of witness that had a pretty significant positive effect on me when I was still trying to figure all this out for myself. And though I can certainly understand whatever ambivalence you may be feeling about this, I am grateful for those who can live *it* and say *it* well.

Living It

His name was Jerry. Jerry was a QC guy on one of the final assembly lines in our factory. All I knew of Jerry in my "pre-Christian days" was that he was a fast walker and was almost irritatingly cheerful. He would say "good morning" to people who walked by his desk. He smiled broadly. He was perky and happy. He was one of those guys who didn't need a cup of coffee to wake up. He was just "high" on life. He never really talked about God (that I can remember). I wouldn't have guessed him to be a religious person, because he was just way too happy for that.

He was a normal guy. He enjoyed fishing. He always had a good story about what he did over the weekend. It wasn't ever off-color, and it wasn't really about religious stuff either. He may have mentioned working with teenagers, but it wasn't in a braggadocios sort of way. He just fit in—sort of. The best way to describe it is that he was just a really good guy. So you can imagine my surprise when I ended up in a living room in someone's home and discovered that he was the one leading the Bible study.

In the middle of all my questioning and wondering about what I wanted to do and who I wanted to be, I was invited to a Bible study. The gal who invited me was attractive, so I thought, *What the heck—it can't hurt. One Bible study won't kill me.* So I showed up at this house. When I arrived, I was about fifteen minutes late. And there were all these teenagers sitting around in a living room. I had been out of high school for over a year. I thought I was way too cool for these people. But my brother, who happened to be sitting on the other side of the room (next to the girl who had invited me), stood up and said, "Hey guys, this is my brother—who we have been praying for!" There were all these knowing grins around the room, and I knew at that point there was no escaping.

I can't tell you anything Jerry said that night, but I do remember thinking to myself, *Ah yes, all this makes sense now. This guy has a reason for being who he is. It isn't about genetics or personality. This is about what he believes. This is about values and faith.* And surprisingly enough, I found myself thinking that I might like to be a little bit more like Jerry. If my life looked more like Jerry's—that might not be such a bad thing after all. In fact, it might be a rather good thing.

People who want to extend to others what God has graciously given to them, have something to learn from Jerry. I don't know how strategic Jerry was about what he did and the way he did it. But I certainly appreciated his approach.

I think some people think that if they really want to make an impact in the world spiritually, then the best way to do so is to have "spiritual" occupation—to come out of the world (so to speak) and become a pastor or leader inside the Church. And yes, God does lead people to do that—and I can celebrate that. But I am absolutely convinced (and unfortunately this isn't talked about enough around the Church) that God "calls" people into the marketplace to live as authentic Christ-followers in the schools, on the police force, in politics, as business owners, financial advisors, real estate agents, and factory workers. There is a calling to be "in" the world. Jesus prayed for this:

> "I'm not asking you to take them out of the world, but to keep them safe from the evil one. They do not belong to this world any more than I do. Make them holy by your truth; teach them your word, which is truth. Just as you sent me into the world, I am sending them into the world." John 17:15–18, NLT

When a person is living out their faith "in the real world" as Paul describes in Colossians 3:12—*clothing oneself with compassion, kindness, humility, gentleness and patience*—it becomes a very compelling witness! It comes across as authentic. It creates real curiosity, because it is sincere. The person watching is left to ponder, why is this person really like this? And in many cases, the only reasonable conclusion is that they are the way they are because their faith has shaped them into *this* kind of person. That kind of "faith-sharing" becomes a very hard example to refute.

Saying It

Now some people—either out of fear or because of negative experiences—prefer to end the discussion with the living piece. They might say things like, "I will live it, and I'll let the preacher man talk about it." But a genuine believer understands there comes a time when a friend, colleague, or family member will need to hear about faith and why it matters—and they will hear it best from *them*. The Scriptures admonish people of faith to be ready for that moment.

> *Always be prepared to give an answer to everyone who asks you to give the reason for the hope that you have. But do this with gentleness and respect.* 1 Peter 3:15, NIV

So when that day comes, what should someone say? Knowing what to say and how to say it is complex. Is it about being overt and confrontational? Does it mean you need to start thinking about walking around with a placard? Is it about standing at street corners and handing out leaflets? How does this really work?

Given the attitudinal shift that is happening in our culture, it serves us well to think long and hard about how to share the life-changing message of Christ. If effectiveness matters, then it would be worth understanding what is happening in our culture and frame the conversation against this backdrop. A book I have found particularly helpful is *Finding Common Ground* by Tim Downs. One of the most powerful takeaways from this book is the idea that there is significant groundwork that should be done before matters of faith are introduced into a conversation.

We are not simply "harvesters"; we must also be "sowers."
By sowing I mean the slow gradual behind-the-scenes work
that prepares a listener—or an entire culture—to be able to
hear the gospel. —Tim Downs

In addition—admittedly, it sounds almost silly to have to say
this, (because it seems so obvious), but I am not sure that it is—it
actually does matter if you care about the person you are talking
to, too. If the attempt to "share the Gospel" is about fulfilling a
religious assignment or obligation, it just doesn't seem to go that
well. It comes across as forced and inauthentic. That kills the deal
even before it gets started. If a Christian can't genuinely find a
reason to care about a person as a person (which might point to a
deeper and more troubling issue), the Christian might want to think
twice before talking about God.

But let's say someone is sincerely interested in learning how
to talk about their faith and they want to do so sensitively and
compellingly. What does that look like? What does the spiritual-
seeking friend need to hear?

I think this is a very individualized matter. It is about answering
questions honestly and candidly. If you don't know—you don't
know! Humility is critical. People don't need to be impressed by
how much you think you know. In fact, don't be afraid to talk
about what you don't know. You don't have to try to be the resident
expert on all things spiritual. Don't be afraid to talk about your
own shortcomings, either. You don't have to have it all together.
Admitting such does not do damage to the credibility of the
message you have to share. It may even enhance it. Besides, it's true.
Being willing to admit to what you don't know and that you are still
figuring things out respects the complexity of what we are talking
about. It engages people in a way that best reflects the manner of
Jesus—who is, of course, the One you are trying to introduce.

I have had the good fortune of serving alongside a very gifted
musician for almost my entire tenure at Woodcrest Chapel. We
have worked together since 1996. He is not only an extremely

talented artist, but he is a great thinker and an equally creative communicator. We have spent many hours talking about the means by which Christians can be more effective at sharing their stories. He regularly elaborates on the fact that every story reflects the love of Christ in its own unique way—we need not try to sugarcoat or exaggerate it. Grace shines best through a transparent vessel.

That said, Chris also suggests that there are probably three characteristics that every seeking person needs to see in and through a story in order to find it engaging and compelling. First, seeking people want to know—and probably need to see—that one's faith really matters. Don't hear *fanatical*. But faith can't be peripheral, either. It must have high personal relevance, and if the seeker can't see that or sense that, then the spoken words (no matter how eloquent) will fall on deaf ears.

Second, they have to have a sense for how faith works. A person listening to a friend expound on their faith is paying special attention to the intersecting points between faith and life. How does faith affect daily decision-making in the areas of parenting, business, entertainment, studies, budgeting, etc.? The question isn't so much about technique as it is about outcomes. They tend to be curious about whether or not a person's faith actually has a positive net effect on the nitty-gritty details of life. If not, then we are just talking philosophy, and most people don't really have much time for that.

The final all-important question is about how faith actually changes someone's life (hopefully for the better). Everyone has some area of their life they are trying to change. People want to be better parents, better employees, better bosses, better spouses, and take better care of their bodies. The bustling self-help sections of bookstores are evidence of this desire. The problem is that changing anything about one's life is actually very difficult to do—so the degree to which faith can help nurture or motivate "real" change becomes an extremely important matter even for the most cynical and skeptical in our day.

The Christ-follower who hopes to capture the imagination

of spiritual seekers has to be able to talk instinctively about soul matters while anticipating these three essential points of curiosity. However, more importantly, I would suspect that most Christ-followers aren't just interested in increasing their effectiveness quotient in any given interpersonal encounter. Rather, they aspire to live a life that authentically reflects the heart and life of Christ as an ongoing and ever-increasing reality. This is a much broader and complicated issue, because it is about full-life stewardship.

And how do we know what that really means?

Leveraging It

Full-life stewardship is ultimately about finding convergence, and convergence is where everything that I am makes sense with everything that God is asking of me.

Wrapping our minds around that reality is a lifelong journey. This isn't something that typically gets answered in a single place or at single time. Some people may talk about lightning bolts and epiphanies—and they may be part of the process—but those are few and far between. Rather, God's purposes are typically revealed progressively over time and in many different places and confirmed by God's Spirit and the community in which He has placed us. It also happens rather haphazardly. It doesn't happen in a linear fashion. I love the statement Annie Dillard made famous:

God draws straight with crooked lines . . .

However, in order to talk about this meaningfully, it might be helpful to reference common processes that tend to play out in certain ways for most people. The illustration I find most helpful is to think about this as though you are going through a funnel. If we at a coffee shop and I had a napkin and a Sharpie, I'd begin drawing again.

At the top of the funnel, we are dealing with broad principles, practices, and processes that are relevant for everyone on this path, but then as we move toward the bottom, we are talking about something very personal and specific—that has certainly drawn from what has gone before, but is nonetheless very individualized! The closer we get to the bottom, the closer we get to convergence.

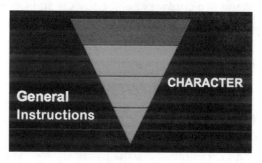

At the top of the funnel we have the *general instructions* that come to us primarily through the Scriptures. God purposes for us individually will not run contrary to what He has already stated in Scripture—this has relevance across the board. So if you are early on in the journey of discovering God's purposes for your life, it may be very much oriented around your *character* and who you are becoming on the inside and what matters most to you. And this is not a small matter (not insignificant or elementary), because strong character is a precursor to whatever it is that God might be calling you to do. Without character, we can sabotage our own success.

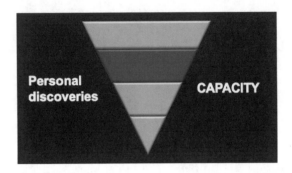

At the next ring we can *discover* spiritual gifts, personality type, and your God-given passion. In short, we learn about our *capacity*. Every Christ-follower has a unique way to reflect God in the world. They have been entrusted with certain spiritual gifts. We all have a have a God-given passion—and it is what you truly care about. It's also wise to consider personal style and one's structured/unstructured, people/task orientation.

This process can be very interesting and energizing, but it only actually raises our awareness about what we *can* do—it doesn't actually help us *do* anything or experience the benefit of doing anything. It is all still theory.

But it does introduce us to the next ring in the process, which is all about *strategic experimentation*. It is not haphazard volunteerism, but strategic experimentation. Armed with the knowledge you have gleaned from the previous two seasons, you can begin to make investments in places that you think might match what you are learning about yourself. This is about discovering the *context* for service. It is about understanding fit.

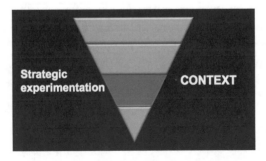

What is so essential about this stage of the process is that everyone must personally own the responsibility of follow-through. I wish that this was less complicated. I wish that there were administrative processes that made this easy for everyone. But people are busy and systems are imperfect. What I have noticed over the last thirty years is that people will be rather enthusiastic about follow-through on those first two rings, and then they get stuck. They try something and it doesn't feel right. It doesn't work out. Somebody doesn't call them back. They experience a relational meltdown with another volunteer. They disagree with the way that certain things are done. Everything comes to a screeching halt.

I think the reason this becomes so frustrating for some people is because they think that others have it easier—and that they are personally being singled out and being put on some list that is designed to keep them out of the game. Now, if you're a jerk and think you know more than everyone else and you can't be a team player, maybe that's true. But I would say that is the rare exception. What is actually more likely is that God has a curriculum for you in the process. There are spiritual tests related to your diligence on these matters, and God wants to build stamina and perseverance in you—because that will be required if you ever want to know true convergence.

The next ring is all about *clarification.* You understand the kind of character that is required and you are growing in that regard. You are becoming increasingly confident about capacities and leaning into them. You have taken responsibility to find the right context, submitting to the people and processes that are part of that context and engaging in the conflict that is necessary to play on that team. All of that is good. But convergence doesn't happen without ongoing tweaks and adjustments. And this is about the *perfecting of your heart and skill.*

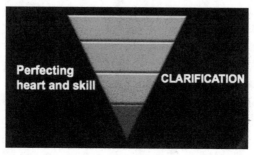

Finding convergence around God's purposes for your life is really about long haul soul management. And candidly, I don't even like that word so much because this is actually about something that God does in us with our cooperation—and "management" sounds like something we initiate. But fundamentally, it is about developing a kind of personal sensitivity where in cooperation with God's Spirit who is at work in you, and in consultation with mentors and leaders you respect, you begin to pay close attention to the finer nuances of what is happening inside—both that which will keep you from being as effective as you could be and those things that would allow you to multiply your effectiveness.

Of all the things that I have talked about thus far, I think this clarifying phase is the most mysterious. This is all about the art of awareness. It is all about honesty and looking at the hard stuff. It is about owning your brokenness and seeking out healing for it. It is about stepping to the plate when you know something more is being asked of you and getting what you need. It is about taking extended times away with God, and it is about going back to school. It is about doing the risky thing you'd rather not do, and it is about letting people see what you would rather not let them see.

It is what Jesus described as the hardest part of discipleship. It is about truly picking up the cross (your cross) and following Him (see Matthew 10:38). It is the end of the life you thought you would be living and the beginning of the life He has marked out for you. It is both dangerous and delightful—all at the same time.

I suspect that if you thought you were being asked to do this alone, you'd be right in saying, "I can't do *that!*" But the good news is that this is why we talk about this in the context of community.

There are many Christ-followers who are on this same journey. There are people who can be of help to you and there are people whom you can help. And as cheesy as this may sound, I am actually quite serious when I say it. Together we can do this.

Final Appeal

I have not forgotten the reader who is still not sure about all of this—the one not yet convinced that Christianity is actually the best way to experience soul evolution. I commend you for hanging with me. Let me close with one final appeal to you.

Every once in a while I have an opportunity to sit across from wise people who are gracious enough to share their insights on life with me. Several years ago, I sat across the table from one such gentleman and I knew enough about his life to know that he had been successful in almost every way you'd measure success. He was married to the same woman for over fifty years. He made a valuable contribution on the job. He worked for the same company from his youth and was highly respected by all who knew him. He designed cutting edge X-ray equipment and had several patents to his name. He had five children, each of whom made their own unique mark on the world. If I mentioned to you his name, you probably wouldn't know him. He never made the headlines. He never really craved attention. He was just one of those ordinary people who lived a good life, enjoyed the simple things, and made the most of the opportunities he was given.

On the day I sat down with him, I had a very specific question I wanted to ask. We chatted for a while over coffee and a piece of apple pie (he had a soft spot for sweets), and then I asked him my question: Of all the accomplishments he had known in his life, which was he the most proud of and why? Or, to put it differently: "*What was the best thing about his life?*"

He thought for a moment, took a sip or two of his coffee, and said, "I think the best thing about my life is that I have no regrets. I haven't lived a perfect life, but I think I got the most important things right. I gave myself to the things I loved, and I think they mattered. Should I die tomorrow, I would feel really good about the life I lived."

It was a great answer. It caused to me to think—and think a lot! I rolled the response around in my mind for several weeks. I tried to imagine how good it would be to be able to say that about my life. How cool would it be to be able to sit in front of an eager student who was wanting to learn the secret to success, and then be able to say, "No regrets!"

WOW!

It was a great answer for him, but it was an answer that haunted me, because I wondered if I would ever be able to say that. I would love to. But when I think back on my life, I have to acknowledge that I have some pretty big regrets. I wish I had done things differently. I wish I hadn't hurt people as deeply as I hurt them. I regret that I didn't take advantage of certain opportunities when they presented themselves. I regret that I let my fears and insecurities get the best of me more than I care to admit—and I am not just talking about the stuff that happened long ago before I supposedly knew better. I am talking about things that happened last month.

I do realize that every one of those disappointments and mistakes created learning opportunities. I think I can take something valuable away from even the most painful memories. But the lessons I learned didn't negate the depth of the regret I still feel. I still wish I had done some things very differently. I know many people who feel the same way. We all wish we could say that we have "no regrets"—but it just isn't very honest.

But what are we going to do?

Wallow in what we should have done differently?

That is one option, I suppose.

The greatest miracle that has occurred in my life is not that I don't have any regrets; the greatest miracle in my life is that I am not crushed by the weight of them. The grace that I have found in the forgiveness that was won for me at the cross of Jesus Christ is such a profound spiritual reality that I cannot imagine what life would be like without it.

Perhaps you can manage living life without experiencing this kind of grace; I just don't know why you would want to.

CONCLUSION

CONFIRMATIONS

Twenty-four hours after I finished the manuscript, I got a call from my mom that my dad had died in a boating accident.

I finished the manuscript on a Wednesday, right at noon. It was an odd feeling really. I had given so much time to this project, but once it was finished I was alone in my familiar easy chair with my computer on my lap. I had emptied my soul on to a keyboard. I had expressed everything I knew (and felt deeply) about God and what it meant to live with him and his people. The completion of the project seemed to merit fireworks or at least a high-five from somebody.

Nothing.

Then came Thursday morning, I got up longing for a way to express gratitude for what I had just experienced—the privilege of having had the chance to do what I had just done. Who gets the chance to take an extended period of time to write thoughts on God? Who gets to stay in a wonderful condominium in the mountains of Colorado to write a book? So many people made this possible. Friends prayed for me. Family supported me. Our church had released and blessed me. Above all, the Spirit of God had sustained and inspired me. My heart was full of wonderful thoughts and a deep sense of satisfaction. I certainly felt blessed beyond what I deserved.

I decided to take a morning bicycle ride along the river that runs through Steamboat Springs. The air was crisp, and the sun was strong. While riding on the path, I thanked God for the life I was living. I thanked him for the blue sky. I thanked him for the puffy white clouds. I thanked him for the laughter of children playing in the fields. I thanked him for the health I had to pedal hard. I thanked him for the truths that I had just finished writing about. I thanked him for the hope that these words might inspire others.

It is hard to describe the sense of fullness that infused my soul.

I got back to the condominium just before noon. My phone had three messages from my mom. When I listened to them, I was stunned. "Piet, please call me! Your dad went sailing this morning and the Coast Guard found the boat, but he was not in it. Call me. Please pray!" I called and we prayed. *O God! Please have mercy.*

If you ever have to wait on news of this magnitude, every minute feels like an hour. You want to call people, but you don't want to burden them. I kept trying to reassure myself that everything would work out. It would be okay.

An hour later, they found his body four miles off shore. He had apparently fallen off his boat and drowned. He was eighty-two when he died. A sailor. A wonderful father of five. An engineer. A man deeply loved by those who knew him.

I was shocked. What a dramatic shift in emotions. I called my siblings. Through our tears we made plans to go directly to Florida to be with my mom. I called the office and asked them to send out an e-mail to our prayer team. I called my sister so that we could meet in Denver to fly out together. My wife called our children and we made arrangements to be together as soon as possible.

As I was packing, I felt numb. I would put something in the suitcase and wondered if I really needed it. I had internal debates about the craziest things. I felt like I was moving in slow motion. But I was actually frantic. We had a short window of time to catch the plane, and I couldn't afford to dilly-dally. The three-and-a-half-hour drive to the airport seemed to take forever. I couldn't believe this was happening.

I met my sister at the gate—which in itself was no small achievement. Denver's airport has two entry points and I almost made the wrong turn, but I felt prompted to go to the left. It turned out to be the right call. The security screening area was packed. But just as I got at the end of the line, they opened another section. Somehow I made it through in five minutes. When I got to the gate area, I discovered that my sister and I weren't sitting together. When I explained the situation to the flight attendant, they moved us together to economy-plus (no upgrade charge).

It was a quiet flight to Orlando. My sister and I would periodically look at each other and tears would fill our eyes. We held hands. We talked about what might have happened to dad. We shuddered at the thought of his drowning. We tried to prepare ourselves for the days ahead.

When we finally made it to my mom's condo (just after 2:30 a.m.), we found the priest and his wife (from my mom's church) waiting up for us. They didn't want my mom to be alone. They had been with her all evening. I was touched by their kindness and sensitivity.

By 4:00 the next day the family was all together.

I have a brother who lives in Hawaii who works on a cruise ship. He happened to be on his thirty-day break, so he could come without missing work. I have another brother who was in Alaska on a cruise with his family, and the cruise line went to extraordinary lengths to make sure he could get to Florida as quickly as possible. My youngest brother was also getting ready to go on a family vacation (so they had already made arrangements for pets, mail, etc.), so they just cancelled their plans, piled in the minivan, and drove all night to be there. Within twenty-eight hours of hearing the news we arrived from the far corners of the country to comfort and console my mom and each other.

Within hours of our arrival, flowers and food began to arrive at the front door. We got e-mails and texts from friends and family far and wide. Later that day relatives from Holland arrived. My mom leads a Bible study in her condominium. Ladies from the Bible study arranged for several of the empty units in the building to be used by family members so that they wouldn't have to incur the expenses of a hotel.

On Saturday afternoon, I got a call from my creative arts pastor. He said, "Lori and I are here in Florida. We just want you to know that we are here, that we love you, and we want to do whatever we can do to help and serve. If there is something we can do just ask." As it turned out, the organist from the church (where we were going to do the funeral) was on vacation, and so Chris's presence was serendipitous indeed. But I was just flabbergasted that he was there at all. Would I have made the trip had our roles been reversed?

On Sunday, we had a memorial service on the beach where they found my dad's boat. As we walked out of the parking lot onto the shore, we just so happened to meet the lifeguard who discovered my dad's sailboat. He told us the story of watching it come into shore. They blew their horn and whistles. But when there was no response, they knew something was wrong. When the boat came aground, they looked inside, and when no one was on board, they immediately called the Coast Guard.

It was a clear day. The surf was light. They found his body quickly. He was floating on top of the water despite the fact that he wasn't wearing a life vest. That is unusual. But we were all grateful for Providence. We tried to imagine what it would have been like to be here today without their having found the body. We expressed our deep appreciation for his fast action and the work he did to try to rescue my dad. He expressed his sorrow over the outcome.

Sunday night I got a call from a friend who was on vacation in Italy. He was actually on a friend's boat in the Mediterranean. He was calling from a satellite phone. I could barely make out what he was saying. The call was breaking up. But, I did understand this much: "Hey, Piet, so sorry about your dad! Do I need to get on a plane and come over there? 'Cause, you know, I would be there in a heartbeat!" He would have. I assured him we were going to make it, but his love and friendship was a gift I cherished—now more than ever.

On Monday morning, I got up to get my mom the newspaper (to make sure they got the details right for the funeral service). I found it on the doorstep on top of a box of donuts. This was the fourth morning in a row there had been donuts on the front porch. When I brought them in, I asked my mom who the donuts were from. She just smiled and said it's our "donut angel." It was the first time I had seen her smile since I had been there. Apparently, she had run into the neighbor a few days before, and he asked if we received the donuts he left. My mom assured him that we were all enjoying them—especially the kids. He said, "Sometimes it is hard to know what to do for people in times like this. But everybody can do something." For seven days in a row we found donuts by the front door.

The funeral service itself was full of depth and meaning. Things were said and done that perfectly honored the life of my dad. It was just right. It is hard to say that funerals are ever a "good" experience, especially when you are dealing with an unexpected and sudden death, but there are times when the experience captures what is needed in the moment, and this was one of them.

The next day, we rented a pontoon boat and spread my dad's ashes on the water. My mom, a pillar of strength, said these words:

"On most occasions like this people would say from ashes to ashes and dust to dust. From the earth we came and to the earth we must return. But those words would not have fit this man. He was a man of the water. This man loved to sail. It was his greatest joy. It is on the water he found his greatest joys. It was on the water he met with God. So, it is to the water he must now return."

She poured the ashes into the water followed by a trail of red roses. It is a scene I will never forget.

We all cried and held each other.

These are the moments when life is hardest. It is when we fully recognize the frailty and brevity of life. We feel vulnerable and alone. We feel shaken and unsettled. We feel the presence of our souls and hope and pray that they are developed enough to see us through.

Through this experience I realized afresh that it is possible to discover a kind of settledness that runs deeper than the pain. For fifty-two years I have been trying to get my arms around that presence. For the last two years I have been trying to find the words to describe it. But, now—in these moments—I was experiencing it. I had seen it and felt again in real life…

In the whispering of the Spirit to make the left turn at the airport…

In the graciousness of the flight attendant on our plane…

In the tender care of the priest and his wife for my mom…

In the tears of family members unashamed of their feelings…

In the extra-mile love of my creative arts pastor…

In the providence of a body found in the ocean…

In the call from the Mediterranean…

In the actions of a donut angel…

In the story of a life well-lived…

In the roses on the water…

Life is unsettling, but it need not remain so.

"Our soul is not at rest until it finds its rest in thee…"
—Saint Augustine